IT'S NOT ABOUT THE TECHNOLOGY

Library of Congress Cataloging-in-Publication Data

A C.I.P. Catalogue record for this book is available
from the Library of Congress.

ISBN 0-387-23350-4   e-ISBN 0-387-23552-3   Printed on acid-free paper.

Printed in the United States of America.

9 8 7 6 5 4 3 2 1   SPIN 11318330

springeronline.com

IT'S NOT ABOUT THE TECHNOLOGY
Developing the Craft of Thinking for a High Technology
Corporation

RAJ KARAMCHEDU

 Springer

To:
My parents and family.
And to my beloved Euni Yim.

CONTENTS

PREFACE

This book attempts to answer the question: "What is that mindset, that particular kind of thinking, that is required of us to be successful in a high technology company *and why?*"

To be sure, the "high" in the high technology does not accord the company any special place in the market. But a unique ingredient distinguishes a high technology company: the culture of innovation that leads to new, often highly complex, technologies. The flip side of this unique culture is the excessive fixation of these companies on the technology superiority. The baggage of this excessive fixation has quite often led these companies to disconnect from the end customer, unwittingly so. Hence our question and this book.

A series of semiconductor startup experiences spurred me to write. The bizarre life in the high technology profession, always precariously disconnected from the world at large, provided the problematic. And a rush *to connect back* lead to *this* book.

If you are not careful, this profession can make you feel isolated from the rest of the world. What starts off as a genuinely rewarding career of learning new technologies, creating new designs, coming up with products that people liked and bought, can quickly turn into a schizophrenia of a respectable sort. How we purport ourselves at work, the extreme stress we undergo to achieve that teamwork spirit, the unending project deadlines that we are always scrambling to meet, seem to put us on a tangential path from the every day life of our families, our children and parents. When this happens, the disconnect is near-complete.

Truly great corporations have become so by attending to this single trait. Leadership at these companies, at every level up and down the hierarchy, are unusually sensitive to this disconnect. Genuinely spirited startups are this way. But these sensibilities do not come packaged in best practices, nor found in the quality assurance manuals. None of this is part of any engineering or business school curriculum, at least not in a way that is impressive. Perhaps the simplicity of this sensibility is not rigorous enough to be included in the academics.

On the contrary, these sensibilities are a direct manifestation of a particular kind of mindset of a few random individuals. Drawn from their own personal experience, these leaders often are not, at first, conscious of the culture they germinate. Nor do they consult manuals to cross-check if their thinking is correct.

This book is an attempt to record the *makings* of such a mindset. More important, we aim to establish *why* the thinking must be in a such a way.

To be sure, you are not ready to write until you overcome the influence of all your favorite authors. And when the topic of your writing is centered on high technology business, it is all the more important to anchor the book in hard reality.

Strictly speaking, a whole of my experience and thoughts have gone into writing this book. However, a few books stand out as the key inspiration. The notion of opportunity cost is drawn exclusively from James M. Buchanan's classic, *Cost and Choice, An Inquiry in Economic Theory*. The notion of economic value add is drawn directly from *The Quest for Value, A Guide for Senior Managers*, by G. Bennett Stewart, III. Almost sixteen years ago at a local book store in Hyderabad, India, where I was born and lived until 1991, I bought that little gem of a book from Fontana Press, George Steiner's *Heidegger*. But it is only after I attended Professor Thomas Sheehan's short course on the same topic at Stanford in early 2003, that I felt as if I was beginning to understand. In many ways, the thinking that is explored in this book runs runs right through all this education, through Hernando de Soto's *The Mystery of Capital*, and comes to fruition in the high technology corporation.

In all my fifteen years of professional life, everyone I interacted with have been kind and helpful to me. They are my context. To that *human connection*, I am deeply thankful.

A few individuals made a direct contribution to the progress of the book. Early spring of 2003, Tim Erjavec, with whom I worked at the semiconductor startup Chameleon Systems, pointed the way and encouraged me to try to keep the writing to a few "timeless" essentials, when I was bogged down with the details. Jim Bland, who exemplified a genuine leadership at Systemonic, Inc., another chip startup I was part of, graciously reviewed the early draft.

Right from day one, Sachin Gangupatula, a friend I've known for nearly fifteen years, encouraged me in a real way. Without his diligent review of those haphazard early drafts, this book would have stayed in the draft stage even now. Numerous conversations with the Tyrrell family, especially Dennis, helped keep the runaway high technology complacency in check. Jose Villafuerte provided useful comments on an early draft. Sreela Sarkar added her perspective in her review. Sean Lorre of Springer saw the merit in my proposal and brought this book to a reality in the marketplace. I hope this book is worth the money you paid for and the time you spent reading it.

PART 1

THE THINKING

1

THE PROBLEM

Consider the following two scenarios:

SCENARIO #1:

The product development is in full swing. The marketing group is reasonably successful in engaging a handful of customer prospects. Beta programs with OEMs are underway and the bill-of-material is nearly finalized. Customer experience with the performance of the preliminary product, albeit at a minimized functionality, is positive. Cautious optimism interspersed with pensive hope mark the moods of designers and marketers, the people close to the product and the customer. Then, with no forewarning a beta customer springs a surprise news. They plan to do a "live demo" at an upcoming tradeshow. However, the product is not yet in a shape for the customer alone to carry on with the demonstration. So they ask for a detailed technical support for two weeks culminating in the tradeshow.

At this stage the support pipeline is already full and the engineering group has no time. As it is they are scrambling to meet the deadline for the final product release. So they resist any diversion of the resources from the development effort and refuse to lend any hand to the customer. The marketing group, however, believes this customer is a high-volume prospect. In their view the company should support this customer at any cost and would not have any such push-backs from engineering.

The ensuing lengthy discussions between engineering and marketing soon turn into heated arguments. Emails start flying back and forth with emotions running high. Bitterness, sarcasm, accusations of personal attacks from one side and posturing with defensive tactics by the other soon seep into the communication.

The CEO, who initially watched from the sidelines, steps in with a mediatory tone, shuffles back and forth between engineering and marketing to quell the storm. But when his soft approach does not help, soon he himself turns aggressive, promising to "kick someone's rear end" and straighten things out.

Regardless, it gets worse as the threats only made the already tired, overworked engineering team discouraged and testy. Eventually the company decides to support the customer after all. However, the response at the tradeshow is disappointing. Due to last minute scrambling of the resources the support team couldn't show a "live demo." Even as they improvised at the tradeshow booth to make the best of it, the thought kept lingering in their mind that if only they had more time to work on the demo setup, and not got sucked into the distractions of the internal conflict.

Worse, this episode distracted the engineering group from its main focus on the final release, resulted in another slip in the product release, and not only scarred the relationship with this beta customer, but put the *entire* business prospect at risk almost overnight.

SCENARIO #2:

A product manager learns from the customer of a competitive feature that will significantly help to keep the product competitive. He turns to the engineering manager with a request to include this feature. However, to the engineering manager, it is infeasible to accommodate this feature addition into the project plan and this late stage. As a conseqence, he pushes back.

More often than not, a deceptively straightforward occurrence such as this soon becomes a hot button issue. Soon both the managers are in a room trying to convince the other of his point of view. The product manager is frustrated as it eludes him completely as to how the engineering manager fails to see such an *obvious* point and what on earth is making him resist the idea.

The engineering manager, on the other hand, sees no reason why he should entertain such a discussion at all in the first place. For him, the schedules are locked in, priorities are set, costs have been estimated, the budget allocated and his product development targets are set. He sees this new feature request as an unwanted interruption that can potentially derail the entire product delivery schedule.

A series of back and forth meetings take place. Soon the interaction turns antagonistic, driving both the parties to dig in and play hardball. The final outcome is determined by whoever presses hard with his negotiating skills to outwit the other. This exchange leaves both parties wary of ever talking to each other again. And yet this is a surprisingly common occurrence in the day-to-day interaction between marketing and engineering in most high technology product companies.

The above two examples illustrate a weakness at the most fundamental level in a high-tech enterprise: *failure at the execution* leading to missed market window. They bring to light what is without a doubt the most crucial factor in determining the success or failure of the company: the *interaction between marketing and engineering.*

What drives these companies to go down such a self-destructive path?

THE INCREASING GAP BETWEEN MARKETING AND ENGINEERING

Every year thousands of new product design starts are launched in the high technology sector. But only a small fraction of them turn into successful products in the marketplace. For example, in the semiconductor industry, a large bulk of the new design starts never *even* make it past the prototype silicon stage.

In a majority of these instances, the *manner* in which these failures occur become clear only in the aftermath. Either the product is *not* what the customer wanted, or the product *did not arrive in time*, or this product *did not have a compelling advantage* over that of a competitor's.

Whatever the case may be, in all these failures, the causes are concrete: either the product was ill-defined, or the engineering team couldn't make it to work before a specific deadline, or there was not a proper coordination between marketing and engineering. Any or all these reasons could have been present.

If the current trend in United States of increasingly outsourcing the high technology *design and development* roles to overseas teams is any indication, then this coordination gap between the marketing and engineering groups is only *going to increase.*

Nevertheless, the gap between marketing and engineering is hardly only of a geographical nature. To transform a design technology into a successful product, the management must bring together the brilliant but technology-oriented engineering groups and the marketing teams on the same page. Quite often this is the biggest challenge faced by the leadership in any high technology company.

How did we end up here?

How is it that, in spite of making remarkable strides in high technology product design, development and deployment of these products in markets, we are still struggling to create a harmony between marketing and engineering professionals?

The central topic of this book hovers around such questions. As we search for answers, our journey takes us on an exploration of the underlying dynamics behind the execution failures in a high technology company.

2

ORGANIZED BUT DYSFUNCTIONAL

To apply Ronald H. Coase's acerbic remark in his essay *The Nature of the Firm*, that "Economic theory has suffered in the past from a failure to state clearly its assumptions" to a high tech corporation would not be far-fetched. In failing to state the assumptions behind their organization model, these high technology corporations leave a large segment of their employee base wallowing in generalities.

Take a semiconductor company for example, large or small, fabless or fab-equipped. The outward view, the view as seen by the press, the analysts, the industry watchers and young graduates aspiring to secure employment in this sector, of how it is *organized* is the *same* across nearly *all* the chip companies.

All these companies project more or less the same view of how they operate. The marketing group is chartered with the tasks of taking the pulse of the market, setting the market trends, to actively engage the customer to define the requirements for the ongoing product and to figure out what the next killer product might look like. The engineering groups focus almost exclusively on building the product itself, concentrate on the day-to-day research, design, development and productization.

Much of this organization is carved out following largely a garden-variety comprehension – in an almost cookie-cutter like approach – of *what* needs to be done to achieve business goals: if you build a competitive product, deliver a time to market value proposition to the customer and minimize costs, then you are more likely to succeed and there is really nothing more mysterious to this business and that's that.

But is this enough?

THE HYPE

Most engineering minds in high technology corporations impulsively shirk at the mention of the words such as "time to market," "competitive advantage," and "differentiation." For them, these words are nothing but empty, vacuous concepts that do not exist except in the minds of the marketer.

Add to this a pedantic reification of these words by most novice marketers.

If you are an engineer, ask any one of these novice marketers on what differentiation means. He will tell you in how many ways your competitor's product is *different* from the product you designed by clinically comparing the features (which is *not exactly* how one should think about differentiation, as we shall see in the book.)

Often it is difficult to separate this marketer's personal opinions from real customer information. As a result, there is a slow undergrowth of defiance against the marketing profession that is naturally built up within the engineering organization.

THE CREEPING MALAISE

The net effect of all this is an unspoken malaise that is prevalent at these companies. It lies at the heart of the company, in the day-to-day interaction between the cross-functional groups of the marketing, engineering, the operations and the sales. Every day the people who work in these groups are subject to this malaise.

Though hard to capture it into a specific form, this malaise can be seen at play in the ever regressing relationship *between those who build the products – the system architects, the designers, the programmers – and the marketers whose onus is to define, market and sell these products.*

Far more clearly seen when a product fails, a peculiar kind of fear seizes the rank and file of the company. This fear is often accompanied by a forgetting of the capability to make sound decisions. Soon the individuals find themselves waging egotistical turf wars in inter-personal interaction.

Communication often is the first victim of this malaise. Marketers and engineers routinely put the entire businesses at risk by doggedly pursuing their own unexamined views. Decisions on what constitutes the right feature, the right product and the right schedule, are often made oblivious to the dangerous effects of such an insular attitude on the fragile customer relationship.

An inexplicable flippancy frequently characterizes a marketer's view of the engineer's world and vice versa. At a time when the market opportunity windows are closing with a far more rapidity than in the past, the semiconductor industry professionals' obsession with a mere technology superiority seems woefully out of place.

All of this is amplified by an almost schizophrenic tendency of the middle management at these companies. Caught in the paranoia of stagnant careers, the middle management seeks fervently for an equal treatment from the higher level executive management but falls short in conferring the same sense of teamwork to the members of its peer level and understudy groups.

It is often this group of middle-level employees that confuse the hard-to-master decision-making skills for the executive power.

Ultimately, the havoc wreaked by this malaise leads to a slow bleeding of the decision making skills from the rank and file. A systemic reluctance to go beyond the call of the duty creeps in. A culture of awkward abstention from crucial decision making prevails. The employees at these companies dead reckon their way through the maze of the day-to-day busy-ness. When stopped in the middle of the track and be faced with a decision, too often they are caught without any clear cut reference point that helps them take a position.

It is as if the people at the company are each riding a unicycle while juggling balls in the air and suffer from the limited maneuverability of, well, riding a unicycle. Although there is a good deal of meticulous balancing involved, there are too many jerky movements, trying to compensate for the continuously slipping center of gravity. And the funny thing is no one really goes anywhere on a unicycle, at least not far enough to call it much of a progress.

When the employees are caught in this turmoil quite often the battle is brutal. The end result is a slow decaying of the life in the corporation with inter-personal relationships teetering on the edge.

For the executive management no problem poses a more threatening challenge than this creeping malaise.

But what *can* they do? The sheer variety of reasons behind such a malaise can make it impossible to grasp the source of the problem. The easy tendency, then, is to look at the current organization as a whole as a source of the problem and to wonder if a reshuffle might help stabilize. So the management employs various corporate work-life improvement tools such as the team building exercises, career enhancement techniques, crash courses on strategic thinking, vision statements, motivational speaking sessions etc.

But none of these tools seem to intuitively leap out in front of the employees at the time of the need and come to aid them through these situations.

It is because the problem lies elsewhere. Something else is at play here. Something more fundamental.

OUR APPROACH

Our approach in this book is markedly different from what one would expect out of a typical book on high technology execution. Let us explain it.

THE SEMICONDUCTOR COMPANY FOCUS

First, a note on the industry sector focus for this book.

No doubt such execution failures are to be found in *any* high technology corporation, wherever technological innovation drives the growth, so one might be tempted to speak in generalities. Nevertheless any useful discussion of such failures will have to elicit the *specific* ways in which these failures manifest themselves. A mere high level approach from the top will not do.

On the other hand, such an insistence on the specifics almost always requires an explicit focus on a *particular category* of companies. To this end, wherever real life examples and real life companies are discussed in this book, the focus is usually on a semiconductor company, as it is the author's background.

While the lessons learned from this investigation may serve the readers with semiconductor background particularly well, we believe a broader audience will benefit from the emphasis we place on learning *how to think* to avoid such failures.

A LAYERED PRESENTATION

Next, a few words on a particular kind of thinking that we want to follow in this book.

We start our investigation with the following premise: despite that we are here talking about a high technology corporation, *neither the kind of market strategy nor the kind of technology itself matters* that much as far as the thinking goes. This premise runs throughout the course of this book.

With that premise set in the background, the book itself progresses in a two-layered manner, as explained below.

LAYER 1: IT'S NOT ABOUT THE TECHNOLOGY

First of all, we are going to set *aside* the entire aspect of the technology throughout this book. By this we mean that any or all *technical* aspects of the high technology industry are out. No discussions on how the latest semiconductor process technology has radically altered the landscape of computer and the consumer electronics. Nor are we going to dwell on the incredible strides made in the digital communication technologies which are enabling wireless and gigabit internet speeds.

What is left then? With all that technology clutter gone, what emerges in front of us is a clear view of the way we engage and interact with the *results* of the technology: the *products* that we use every day at work and in our homes.

It is at this underlying layer, previously hidden from us, that we find something very interesting.

We find that this underlying layer is a hotbed of value construction. In what way?

First, all that we *do* takes place at this hotbed, though without us being too conscious of it.

Second, and more important, is the role played by *a context.*

We are going to introduce and talk about the phenomenon of context. Whether it is as a consumer or the designer of these products, the *manner* in which we interact with any technology product is a function of *a particular context* we find ourselves in. How we come to associate a particular utility with a particular product, the construction of meanings, the affinities that shape the value of a product, all of it happens in a context. As we lift the veneer of the technology clutter, we are suddenly exposed to this underlying view of a thousand contexts, each of which shapes the perception of what a technology product means to us.

It is a view that also offers something unique to us: it takes our habitual awareness of the economy as this huge, almost undecipherable, nebulous, and a boundary-less blob of a "market force," and breaks it down into a set of a specific human *experiences* that constitute the economic activity.

In other words, this view demonstrates to us once for all that our very *economic activity* is largely driven by the multitude of contexts that we find ourselves in.

ARTICULATION IS HALF THE PROBLEM

As long as we do not comprehend this underlying layer, we are left with nothing but the details of the technology, with the details of a market strategy in which to look for the source of the execution problem. As long as our view of the origins of the economic activity remains *disconnected* from the underlying multitude of contexts, we are forever relegated to the clutter of the technology and the source of the execution problems eludes us.

Why is this so? What do these multitude of contexts have anything to do with the execution problem?

It is our belief that, strange it may seem, the quality of execution is intricately tied to the very economic activity that we all bring about in our everyday lives.

This powerful underlying hotbed of a thousand contexts, that we are about to bring to light in this book, is always present with us, whether we are a consumer or a producer. In fact it is present with us whether we are employed in a high technology company or not.

But, *when placed in the purview of a high technology company context*, this underlying hotbed becomes a fundamental reality that shapes the worldviews, the *actions*, the *decisions* and eventually the *execution performance* of each individual in a company.

As a consequence, we must turn to this company context, this underlying hotbed, to find the source of the execution problem. We predicate our book on the belief that, there *is* indeed this unarticulated reality, hidden beneath the official roles that distinguish the employees from one another. A significant part of our initial focus in this book is in *articulating* this reality.

As we begin to comprehend this underlying reality, the light starts to shine on terms such as "differentiation," "utility" etc., in a unique way. These terms are not just concepts anymore, but unique and basic economic *experiences*. Our understanding of these terms becomes clearly grounded in the context-driven economic activity that we engage in. For example, we demonstrate how the idea of a market differentiation can be thought through in terms of clear and distinguishable occurrences of a human experience, even as we engage in economic activity.

LAYER 2: DEMYSTIFYING EXECUTION

Armed with this new understanding of the contexts, we then take the next step.

Remember that in Layer 1 we peeled off the outer layer of the technology and dug into the underlying layer. Now we go back. However, this stepping back does not return us to the technology level, but takes us to a space in which the day-to-day practice of execution takes place. Not surprising, considering that our whole investigation is centered on the experience of the individual employee in the high technology company.

In this second phase, we undertake the task of demystifying the execution. Throughout this phase, we continuously apply the framework we developed in Layer 1.

BREAKDOWN IN EXECUTION

So what can we say about the failure of the execution?

The reality in which the high technology company's day-to-day execution takes place is a microcosm of the decision making, the mutual agreements and mutual dissents among people of diverse backgrounds and perspectives. It is a vibrant playing field with a variety of contexts in which the engineering and marketing groups find themselves even as they engage each other in various joint projects to achieve corporate goals.

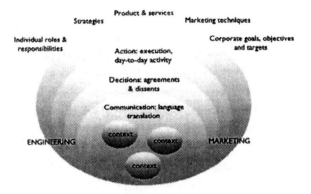

Microcosm of a High Technology Corporation

This microcosm is marked by the difference in the languages spoken by these two groups, the ensuing challenges in the communication, the agreements and dissents which motivate the actions of the individuals.

When viewed in this manner, the *execution* aspect boils down to three factors: understanding the context, choosing the relevant information and making the right decision in a timely manner.

We believe that it is the break down of these three factors that constitutes the break down of the execution. The failure to understand the context, hanging to an irrelevant piece of information either because of its strength of appeal or because it is one's own opinion and finally the fear of making the decision, are the manifestations of this breakdown.

EMPHASIS ON THINKING LIKE A MARKETER

Then, what about the interaction between marketing and engineering groups? If the gap between marketing and engineering were to be the result of only a lack of understanding of the marketing *processes*, then our task would be easier. Just provide an overview for a set of standard marketing practices, tools and techniques as they pertain to high technology marketing and that should suffice.

But as we observed earlier, we believe a proper way to close the gap is to provide an insight into how a high technology marketer *thinks*. The standard marketing techniques and practices, while they are useful, are simply the *result* of a particular kind of thinking that a good marketer is attuned to. These standard techniques do not often provide an insight into the actual thinking itself.

Which is where the application of the context framework comes in.

We are interested in showing the underlying thinking behind the high technology marketing *function*. We believe *everyone* in the company should be conversant with this kind of thinking.

After the context framework is fully developed, the focus in this book turns to the day-to-day context of the semiconductor company. The approach we have in mind is to stay close to the ground and chart the gradual progression of a chip company from its initial product conception stage, through an initial customer approval, to a successful design win and finally the delivery of the solution to the customer.

MOTIVATION

Finally, a note on the motivation behind this approach.

If you are an engineer who has just made a career transition into a product marketing role, chances are you will soon realize the following.

First, the specific activities you need to do as a high technology marketer, such as how one goes about defining the product, the mechanics of working towards a design win, what is involved in qualifying a customer, etc., *are not written down* anywhere (though there are good marketing strategy books out there.)

Second, the success of a high technology company is so intimately tied to these specific activities that if you didn't master the skills of how to execute them, at least be aware of them, there is a good chance that your value to the company is minimal.

Therein lay the dilemma. If there is no reference source that tells you what type of skills sets you must develop, what kind of specific activities you need to perform, how to prioritize them, how to make decisions, how to *think like a high technology marketer*, then how is one to know *what* to execute, let alone know how to execute?

Current literature offers no guidance because it talks only about a high-level strategy, not the day-to-day execution. Learning from one's colleagues and peers at workplace should not be the only way around this dilemma.

Hence, a systematic understanding of the high technology execution is absolutely critical to the execution success of the entire company.

NOT A PRESCRIPTION

Although we occasionally provide a few suggestions on what we think is the right way, this book is in no way a prescriptive, a "how to" book. There are no short cuts, no new strategies, no new buzz words.

As a result, the tone and approach of this book is decidely exploratory. What *is* new is the approach to the thinking. This book exposes the reader to the craft of the thinking that is required by a high technology corporation. If we succeed in connecting the key elements of execution into a single framework, naturally we hope to learn new ways of thinking about success.

3

THE AWARENESS OF
AN ENGINEER

We can make a reasonable evaluation of the success potential of a high technology company by looking at how the marketing and engineering groups interact within the organization. More importantly, of the two groups, the perception of the engineering organization is a direct indicator of where the company is headed.

Let us start by asking questions such as: How do engineering groups view the day-to-day business in the chip company? What is their understanding of critical factors for success? What is the level of visibility of these two groups into the other?

Not surprisingly, what we find will depend on the maturity and the leadership of the company. But by and large, whether it is a startup or a large company, we can expect to find varying degrees of interactions between marketing and engineering groups.

In first case, we have instances of engineering groups that have little or no visibility into the workings of a marketing organization.

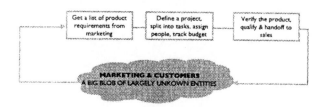

A Nebulous View of Marketing and Customers

In this environment, an engineer's view of what is important to the company and how it is important is more or less along the following lines:

"We have already developed a technical specification for the chip. And there is a document for product requirements that the marketing group has prepared. Between these two documents and the engineering manager's project plan, there is pretty much all that is there to know. Whatever else marketing does is nothing but a big blob of unknown."

For an engineer, *something* happens in the marketing division that eventually equips the marketers with a product requirements document. Ask anyone in the engineering group but there is only a vague understanding of what that something is.

Not all companies are this way, however. In a large majority, the prevalent understanding of the marketing function within the engineering groups is a little more specific and concrete.

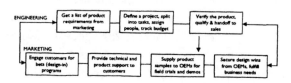

A Better View, But Still Incomplete

Most semiconductor companies that are startups tend to be technology-centric at the beginning. Even though at the executive level the management does have a clear understanding of how business is done, a large number of employees among the rank and file only have a peripheral understanding of how money is made.

Often it is inadequate. Even in this age of customer-centric organizations, a majority of technology-driven semiconductor companies think that it is unnecessary to seek an OEM customer's input during the chip design. The underlying thinking that drives this mindset goes along the following lines:

"Basically our technical people already know what we are building, how we should design it and what the product should do. Isn't that why our company hired them? And our guys are really brilliant people with doctorate degrees and several patents to their name. If you are telling me that a customer can understand what our chip should be, then why don't they build it themselves? Why come to us?"

"Why don't we just build the chip first, and make sure to keep it a secret while we are building it. We release any official information out to public only when we are done. We make a big marketing splash, our sales guys would go get customer orders and we sell our chip. Isn't that why we hire marketing and sales people?"

What is wrong with such a mindset? Why is it important that *everyone* in the company understand the core marketing functions? As a matter of fact, isn't that why we hire marketing and sales people?

Let us witness an imaginary dialogue between a newly appointed CEO and the employees of a semiconductor company to illustrate our point.

ILLUSTRATION

The board of directors of a medium-sized semiconductor company has just hired a new CEO. The company is in a three-year long slump. It has lost the top position in its market segment to an agile competitor 24 months ago and there appears no end to the slide.

The CEO is no stranger to managing companies that have multiple business units and hundreds of products in the market, such as this. So in a first order of tasks, she pulls together the key customer-focused sales and marketing managers into a conference room. Here is the dialogue.

CEO: When I look at the variety of products that we have in the market, I know I ought to feel that is our strength. But we all know we have a problem. Our market share has been shrinking throughout the last eight quarters and the bleeding continues. We have been consistently slipping the product release schedules.

Simply put, we are not getting the kind of revenues per product as we should and as the original business case calls for. We need to figure out if we have to make any changes to our new product investments. Do we have the right set of products? Are we measuring ourselves effectively? What is the problem? Have we lost our customer focus?

BUSINESS MANAGER: I think that most of our focus has been just on the revenue per product. That is the reason why we have so many products. It also could be the source of the problem. We don't seem to study the market before deciding what products we should build.

Funny, even though we have so many products in the market, not many of them seem to speak to what our core competency is. I understand that at the end of the day it is the revenue that matters but competitive advantage of the product is important too. Every product that we make, our competitor is able to imitate, beat us to the punch and take the market-share from us. This needs to be fixed.

SALES MANAGER: I agree with that comment. Also I'll be the first one to admit that we don't have a product strategy. If we look at the number of products we make, they are all over. Each of them seem to come from an engineer's dream and a pet project. Since we ask our engineering groups to innovate, they are innovating, which is a good thing. But we are turning all of these pet projects into products without testing if there is a market for them.

APPLICATIONS MANAGER: I've been with the company for more than 15 years now and I can say that our platform products, the non-ASIC products, are a drain on our sales resources. We spend enormous amounts of time teaching our customers how to use our software. I am in-charge of applications for our Prodigy* platform series (a programmable silicon with an embedded processor.) It takes an average 8-10 weeks for a simple receiver sub-block to be built from ground up, map it onto a Prodigy part and that too with the help of our apps guys! When are we going to improve our software tools? As you know, the customer must have a design closure before they can consider placing a volume order with us.

SALES MANAGER: This is not the first time we've heard that complaint before. I have the same experience trying to sell the Prodigy platform to our east coast prospects. Practically every customer tells us that our software tools don't speak the same language as their system design requires. Worse, there are other tools in the market that do a better job but customers can't map their systems to our parts using these other tools. I am of the opinion that perhaps this platform game is not in our core competency, never was. We should probably rethink this whole thing (once again!).

PRODUCT MANAGER: Let's talk about our system IC products, which are standards-based. Our engineering managers don't seem to understand that slipping schedules are a direct hit on the revenue.

This is a real problem and here is what I mean: when we start a project based on the current standard, whether it is in multimedia or in wireless, we start out with an ambitious plan of a big system-on-chip and we have one or two large customers "committed." But we take so much time to execute!

* A fictitious name

The Omega˙ project is a perfect example in that it took a year *longer* than the original business case projection, and by the time we came out with the chip, the market has already moved into ASSPs for this standard! Now it is hard to compete in the lower-priced ASSP market with such a power-hungry system-on-chip with all kinds of stuff on it. Customer is no longer willing to pay for it! Result? Lower, vastly lower than expected volumes, no pricing power and no new customers for this system-on-chip.

Our problem is exactly this: slipping development schedules and hence missing time to market windows.

SALES MANAGER: I think you've hit the nail on the head with that point on time to market. I don't think there could be much of an issue with the original business plan but as the schedules slip, the market projections go out of the window. It is then hard for marketing to even maintain customer interest when there is no working product as per the original schedule!

In fact I would say that it is not so much the schedule slip that is the problem, although it is a major setback. It is the *uncertainty* as to *when* the marketing will have a working product from engineering. I appreciate the problems the engineering guys face on a day-to-day basis but the unpredictable nature of product availability kills us. Customer cannot plan based on a moving target.

BUSINESS MANAGER: In case of the Prodigy platform-processor product, I have the same reaction from the customer. They told us more than once that our folks who develop the software tools didn't seem to have ever designed a chip in their life. Sorry guys, but this is what I hear. Don't shoot the messenger! They wonder how the requirements process was done for these software tools.

SALES MANAGER: Speaking of requirements and the product definition, I think our product definition process is very engineering-oriented. We start projects based on our own opinions of what is possible and we just do it. The business unit

---

˙ a fictitious name

goes out and gets the product development approval with anecdotal demand numbers and forecast figures. Just like that! It is up to the product marketing to show the customer commitments and usually there is none because it is all premature. Still the project gets approval because it is in the key interest to keep the high profile of the company in the standards bodies.

How are we sales guys expected to sell this product when we don't know why and for whom this product is built? Of course if the standard is there then surely there will be someone who buys this product but that is just an accident, right?

PRODUCT MANAGER: I don't know if my issue pertains to the question you raised but I'll say it anyway. Often times the product slips are caused, I think, significantly due to the endless cycles of discussions and dispute resolutions between the engineering and marketing/sales groups.

Can the executive management come up with a process or a management technique to solve this issue? Engineering always asks us to choose between a feature and schedule. There is always a stock response from engineering: if we ask for a feature they say the schedule will slip by a few months and if we ask the product on-time, they will want to minimize the features so much that the product looks weak even on paper! I think the issues seems to be prevalent in the whole company.

THE "BLOCK-HEADED" THINKING

Nothing in the above hypothetical, but realistic, dialogue suggests that there is a lack of a marketing organization in the company.

But still it is clear that the struggles of this ailing organization are at a basic level: lack of an easy-to-use product, no market driven strategy, a preponderance of engineering projects disconnected from a well-identified market opportunity, slipping product schedules, and lost revenue opportunity.

What is missing? What is it here that is eluding the traditional "best practice" of engineering and marketing organization?

First, the main culprit is the thinking that just like engineering, the task of marketing can also be accomplished by means of a *deterministic process*.

Most technology-driven organizations have a system-level view of the world: capture all the key variables into a black box, set ranges to each such variable, and *pre-set* the input and output conditions. The goal of the company then is expressed as simply taking this pre-defined system-level architecture and building a product out of it.

Most engineering managers do not admit to explicitly adhering to this philosophy but their thinking and the mindset is largely driven by it. The fact of whether the company can then market or sell this product is really a problem for the marketers and sales folks to figure it out. There is even a bemusing "If you can't sell the product we built, then what good are you?" attitude present.

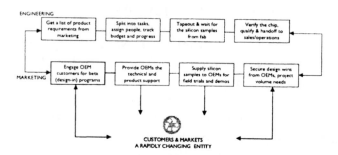

A Market-oriented View

Second, the operating model in the minds of these individuals invariably takes on a familiar *block-oriented* form.

These block-oriented models make us think that the business of high technology is a *logical* sequence of events. There is a definition of a task, a flow of *data,* and a *handoff* point. It looks neat when we draw such block diagrams on a piece of paper.

Perhaps the most important shortcoming in this block-oriented thinking is a complete relegation of the time-to-market factor. The time-to-market factor is an *after the fact* variable. As a result, the prevalent engineering thinking, used to grasping the "big picture" entirety of the project in terms of popular project management tools, considers the time to market constraint as an intrusion in the proper care and development of the product.

This block-oriented thinking encourages a perception that what is to be done can be neatly carved into tasks. Whoever is assigned this task, considers it done when the results are handed off the next link in the chain, and a document is produced showing the work.

Real world markets, on the contrary, rarely provide allowances to products built in such a manner. Markets and customers abhor products that are not shaped by them. Unfortunately, most high technology companies have a blind spot in their thinking that makes them oblivious to the complexities of the markets.

At the same time, just simply knowing that there is a customer, and there is a market out there isn't of much help, although it is an improvement. What is needed is an organization whose mental model of the company is tied to the time-to-market constraints.

4

MARKETING'S CHOICE AND ENGINEERING PLANNING

Our first step in disinterring the underlying reality of the day-to-day execution in a high technology company puts us directly at the center of the execution engine. This is where the worlds of a marketing manager and the engineering manager come in contact with each other.

Although this aspect is never discussed explicitly in this manner, there is an underlying fault-line that is ever present in a high technology company.

No one talks about it, although every one is subject to its influence. Not much is done to rein it in, although in almost every critical activity at the company there is its impression, shaping the contours of the decision process. It strikes at the heart of the day-to-day workings of the company, creating impasses among people, springing up surprising twists and turns in their decision making capability.

This is the fault-line that runs through and divides the worldviews of a marketer on one hand and of the rest of the company on the other. It has to do with the concept of the cost. The subtleties around this largely ignored concept, as far as the term "cost" is deemed a no-brainer, are mostly unspoken and are almost never examined.

A MARKETER'S COST

For a marketer, the concept of a cost is *always* intertwined with the *choice* and *decision making*. In this sense, the concept of the cost in the mind of a marketer is the *opportunity cost*. This opportunity cost is distinctly characterized in the way that it is *not the same* as the traditional definition of the cost.

This is where the fault-line lies. This fault-line separates the conventional understanding of the cost as viewed by the engineering manager in all his calculations of the schedule, time, effort and the resource estimation, from the opportunity cost as viewed by the product marketer.

To be sure, the idea of the opportunity cost is nothing new to the business community. Sales personnel, marketing executives and the venture capital community routinely use this term. It can be found in any basic economics and management textbook. Nevertheless this subtle difference in the interpretation of the word "cost" rarely gets the attention it deserves.

Considering how deeply this difference divides the worldviews of the marketers and engineers, and influences their ability to arrive at a consensus at crucial decision points, it is worthwhile to examine this phenomenon at length.

THE OPPORTUNITY COST

Let us elaborate what opportunity cost means by means of an illustration.

We are all familiar with the normal day-to-day usage of the term *cost*. When we buy a desktop computer at an electronics store, we pay the price of the computer at the checkout counter, and walk out with the box. When someone asks how much it cost us, we mention the dollar amount we paid at the checkout counter. Simple and straightforward as that. It is the outlay, or how much we have expended, what we paid, after we decided to buy that particular desktop computer item we liked on the shelf.

The *opportunity cost*, on the other hand, is slightly tricky.

At the store sure enough there were other items on the shelves that for a moment sparked our interest. For example, there is that brand new IBM laptop, or the new PDA with a built-in camera and an MP3 player or the new tablet PC with a cool handwriting feature.

When we first looked at these items on the shelves we were perhaps tempted, though briefly. But eventually we made up our mind to settle with the desktop computer and decided that's that. The opportunity cost here is the perceived *benefit* we would have enjoyed had we bought that PDA or that laptop or that tablet PC but which we have *chosen to forego*.

Let us reiterate once again that the opportunity cost is *not* the cost, as cost is understood in conventional terms: it is not the cost of that laptop, or that PDA or that tablet PC that we walked away from. Instead it is the *benefit* that we would have enjoyed had we bought any of these items instead of the desktop computer. In other words, we decided to skip the opportunity to buy one of these items, and therefore walked away from the perceived benefits of all these items.

If an observer were to watch our behavior and were to know exactly what was going on in our heads while we made these decisions, to this observer we would appear as if to buy the desktop computer we paid the price through the benefits of all these other things. It costed us all these benefits when we bought the desktop computer. This is the opportunity cost.

A key aspect to underscore is, all these benefits that we have chosen to forego are only the *perceived* benefits because as such we have not bought any of these items to personally experience these benefits. In making the choice, that decision to buy the desktop computer, in our minds we sort of projected forward, judged in our minds, and made an assessment that to us the value of the desktop computer means more than either an MP3-player equipped PDA or the newest IBM laptop.

THE FAULT-LINE

Now let us see how this understanding of the opportunity cost can aid us in deciphering what makes a marketing manager and an engineering manager think differently.

Let us call the space represented by the variety of electronic gadgets on the shelves at the electronic store as an *opportunity space*.

A marketer's worldview starts with this opportunity space.

Imagine that at a certain point of time in the near future there are four products on the shelf: products A, B, C are made by your competitors and product X is made by your company.

So a potential customer who is in the market to buy a product such as the one your company makes, has four choices he could turn to: A, B, C or X. Obviously you want the customer to buy your product X.

A marketer looks at this opportunity space from a unique vantage point. From this view, the marketer is like the detached observer that we referred to above, with a keen eye on the decision making mode the customer is about to enter into. The marketing manager at your company observes the customer in the decision making mode and looks at how he can compete with his product X in the following manner:

This customer would buy X only if he is fully convinced that the perceived benefits of buying either A, B or C are *considerably less* than the benefits he gets if he buys product X. Your marketing guy knows that the customer, thinking along these lines, is on the verge of making a decision.

At the same time, the marketing manager also knows that the customer is nevertheless faced with the dilemma of not knowing exactly if the perceived benefits of A, B, and C are less enough to forego them. Or, to put it conversely, if the value of X outweighs the perceived benefits of either A, B or C.

As it should be expected in situations such as these, now emerges a competitor. For example company A, which makes the product A, decides to tip the scales by providing an additional feature.

When the product strategy in-charge at company A announces the release date of the new product A with this feature included, it has the effect of modulating the opportunity space as viewed by the customer and the whole playing field changes. This is what we call changing market condition.

The customer now sees that his opportunity cost has just increased if he goes with X vis-à-vis product A so he starts to gravitate *away* from the product X. This change of direction in the customer's mind is certainly not good for your marketing manager. The least your marketing manager could do now is first to tip the scales *back* into balance by matching product X with the same feature to reduce the opportunity cost for the customer. Or employ some other strategy that eventually results in tipping the scales back in favor of product X by reducing the opportunity cost for the customer.

In this fashion the marketers are constantly trying to influence the customer by altering the opportunity cost landscape in a manner that forces the customer to align favorably to the product X.

It does not matter if the opportunity space available to customer has three products such as A, B and C or just the product A in addition to your product X. Armed with his subjective judgment on the opportunity cost, the customer is *always* engaged in the assessment of X in the entire opportunity space, to make a decision.

In other words, the marketer of your product is forced to operate in a realm of opportunity cost which is *always* intertwined with the *choice* and *decision making* on the part of the customer.

Unlike the electronics store example cited above where the consumer is often prone to making impulse and sometimes irrational buying decisions, the high technology marketing is much more methodical but equally brutal.

An OEM company, who is typically the customer for the chip vendor, has ample time, sometimes up to a year, to evaluate the chip samples. The beta engagement phase is rather elaborate. The levels of scrutiny the chip product is put through are substantially more and extremely thorough. Add to this an incessant tendency on the part of the OEM customer to dress down your chip product's value so that he can extract lower price.

This is the inescapable nature of the high technology markets, a vast ecosystem made up of sophisticated, thinking, and decision making human beings. They are constantly evaluating what their opportunity costs would be if they select your product. Their decisions can potentially factor you out of the market quite simply and quickly without loyalty, sympathy or emotion but driven largely only by an intangible and highly subjective criterion called the opportunity cost.

THE FAULT-LINE MANIFESTED

Compare the marketer's worldview of the opportunity cost with the engineering manager's view of the cost and we see immediately how the picture changes. For this, we turn to the product development costs we alluded to in the earlier chapter.

A product development project takes on the signs of life usually after a torrent of initial assessment of the markets and products.

This is followed by a preliminary definition of the products that enable the company to enter this market. Project milestones are laid out. A preliminary estimation is made on how long it takes to build the product, how many people it takes, their salaries, the upfront investment for computers, the software tools, usage of the laboratory equipment etc. All of this is rolled into a budget.

The engineering manager's objectives are defined in terms of delivering the product with an agreed set of minimum features, within a given time schedule and under a given budget. All these are the costs that appear in the financial statements of the project. They all can be measured, verified, and tracked for the purposes of budget control.

Recall the scenario illustrated at the beginning of the book where the marketing manager and engineering manager are engaged in a heated discussion on the matter of a certain feature inclusion into the product.

When the engineering manager encounters a request such as this, several factors come into play and motivate him into taking the kind of position he takes.

First of all, the development costs have already been *budgeted*. Extreme care is taken so that all these costs are measurable and trackable. There is a natural controlling purpose that is attached to these development costs and this kicks in immediately. As the request for a feature modification (or a feature change) comes in, the engineering manager instinctively assumes a cost-control mode, tries to *minimize the cost* of the ensuing disruption to the project brought on by this request.

On the other hand, the marketing manager has his eyes cast wide on the opportunity space. He is fixated on managing *down* the perceived benefits from the competitive products. The marketing manager is not looking at the costs of the engineering manager but instead looking at *minimizing the opportunity cost for his customer*. And in this effort to minimize the opportunity cost for the customer there is a tendency to increase the "value" of the company's product (product X in the above illustration.) This feature addition request is meant to achieve that value increase.

This is how the fault-line manifests.

THE COST ASYMMETRY

When we look back at the two colliding worldviews of the engineering and marketing managers, something fundamental stands out and characterizes this fault-line.

It is the role accorded to the subjective individual.

In the world of a marketer, defined by the notion of the opportunity cost, an individual is an integral part of the cost and choice making phenomenon. On the contrary, in the budgetary cost analysis of the engineering planning, there is no room for such a subjective element.

Moreover, if we look closer into this fault-line dynamic, we see that there are a few other aspects of the turmoil between engineering and marketing managers.

First, while the engineering manager's costs are organized, are verifiable and trackable, the marketing manager is faced with a hard-to-quantify measure of the opportunity cost. This is because the opportunity cost is the perceived benefit of the competitor's product in customer's eyes and it is just that, the *perceived* benefit.

As a result, the opportunity cost is a highly subjective entity, sometimes fraught with an arbitrary and an irrational decision making process on the part of the customer.

Second, in executive staff meetings where big decisions are made based on the information available at that time, it is the engineering manager's budgetary cost that is used. The opportunity cost is never even discussed. This is primarily because it is not quantifiable in dollar terms.

As a result of such complete absence of opportunity cost in the decision making, a sort of an *asymmetry* is built into the job responsibilities of the product manager and engineering manager roles. When the senior executive management of the chip company experiences these two worldviews colliding, as witnessed by the CEO in the first scenario illustrated at the beginning of the book, it is mainly as a consequence of this asymmetry.

FAULT-LINE REVISITED

The fault-line described in the earlier section gave us a general glimpse into the choice-making phenomenon that we all experience, though this experience is not explicit. It is indeed true that none of us really are thinking in terms of the opportunity cost when we walk into an electronics store. But the thoughts, the emotions and the subjective evaluations which implicitly drive our decision making, as far as we are engaged in the economic activity of purchasing a product, manifest themselves in a *manner* of the opportunity cost.

Notice that even though there is this fault-line running through the worldviews of a marketing manager and an engineering manager, this fault-line does *not* manifest itself until there is a customer request for a feature enhancement.

But why do we see such seemingly unrelenting requests for feature enhancements from a customer in the first place? For that matter, *why* does a customer choose one feature over another, one product over another?

To say that it is to minimize his opportunity cost would be simply to shift the burden to the next question: "How does a customer *evaluate* these benefits to measure the implicit opportunity cost?"

To say that it is to differentiate would be close. All marketers treat differentiation as a fact of life. In every marketer's worldview, unless you differentiate your product, your service, your message, for that matter *anything* you have to offer, you don't stand a chance to survive.

Differentiation is important not just because it almost single-handedly determines the success or failure of the product in the market place. It is important also because any differentiating feature can only be built successfully into the product by a conscious *joint* decision between a marketing manager and an engineering manager. Not a day goes by without a senior manager wondering if the team fully appreciates the value of a certain differentiating feature in the product.

So, what exactly is "differentiation?" This is the question we tackle in the next chapter.

5

DIFFERENTIATION: A PHENOMENON, NOT A CONCEPT

For most professionals in high technology industry, differentiation is a forced response.

The first time we heard of it, it was more likely presented to us as a necessary evil that we must wrestle with to survive in the "cut-throat" markets we are in. And so we religiously put this acquired skill into practice whenever we break down the products in terms of their features, draw up a nice comparison table and show the superiority of our product over that of the competitor.

For most of us, the manifestation of the differentiation lies in the relative differences between the features of the two products. The ability to claim, "We have a *better feature*" whenever we pull up our presentation foils seems to lodge itself in our minds as the goal we must aim for.

This is a problem.

A prevalent mindset in the high technology industry is the tendency to measure the superiority of a product's feature *in isolation*, blissfully ignoring to elicit any connection whatsoever to the *benefit*. This obliviousness is so rampant that it behooves a serious examination of the root causes of it. We start this chapter with a few preliminary observations on this matter.

A CONCEPT IS IMPERSONAL

Surely it is not the case that we do not comprehend the concept of the benefit. The problem is much deeper. It lies in the way we have been presented the idea of differentiation in the first place. The problem began, way back in the beginning of our professional careers, when we encountered this idea of differentiation *as a concept*. Let us explain what we mean.

The curious thing about a concept is when someone comes up with it for the first time, it is usually announced to a wider audience *as a generalization* of a series of consistent observations. In this sense, the originator offers us these generalized observations rolled into a nice *finished-product* package of the concept, while keeping the ingredients that led to the formulation of it hidden, more often cleaning them out as an unnecessary clutter.

Strictly speaking, you and I don't have to be privy to these behind-the-scenes observations as long as we take the concept at its face value and apply it as recommended. In other words, we don't have to *experience* the same intuition or the same epiphany of the original presenter of the concept, in order for the concept to be true.

Yet, by this same reason of obviating the experience of it, a concept tends to be an abstract quality. By reason of this inherent abstractness it tends to fall outside the realm of human experience. Even if there is no human audience, a concept stands on its own, still true and valid regardless of an individual's comprehension of it.

This is where the problem begins.

Concepts work best when they are about an aspect of a science or a technology, areas where the abstractness goes hand in hand with the intellectualization of it.

To understand what we mean, let us look at an example of the data processing unit in the internal circuitry of the computer processor chip.

A data processing unit at its heart is a concept. It has a deterministic, fixed definition for it. It also has a corresponding reality in the silicon. Very few of us have seen this data processing unit but we know it is there. We don't have to *experience* this data processing unit to believe that it is there, residing in the computer chip.

The efficacy of this data processing unit has nothing to do with the human experience of it. We are all quite happy even if the idea of the data processing unit were to be an abstract one, *outside* of the human experience, as long as it does the job and keeps processing those bits at the breakneck speed that it does.

Differentiation, on the other hand, is the exact opposite.

It lies entirely within the realm of an individual's experience. In this sense, differentiation is a *phenomenon*. It is so intricately tied to the subjective experience of an individual that to grasp the essence of it, we need a different approach. Differentiation requires us to comprehend it not from the finished-product *concept* of it, but from a much earlier stage where the *raw materials* of an individual's subjective experience start to come together to form the essence of differentiation.

THE MISSING DIMENSION: THE *INDIVIDUAL*

A phenomenon such as differentiation is quite unlike that of a data processing unit. It is different in the sense that unless *someone*, an individual, actually feels that difference, is clearly convinced in their minds, the differentiation *will not exist*.

The differentiation is not a physical entity that is manufactured in fabrication plants, put on a silicon chip and delivered to the customer. It cannot show up on its own, nor can it stand on its own. It is a quality that lies entirely *within the subjective world* of the audience to which a product pitch is made. For the phenomenon of differentiation to emerge, it needs a corresponding subjective world in which to emerge in.

Herein lies the root cause of the problem. The problem lies in that when we try to create differentiation by feature comparison alone, we erroneously treat differentiation as a concept. We forget that differentiation requires the subjective world of the customer as a breeding ground for its emergence. We assume that differentiation can stand perfectly on its own, within the relative differences between the features that are being compared, and all we have to do is to highlight these relative differences!

Nothing could be further from the truth.

The high-technology field has become so accustomed to dealing with *technical* concepts and *technical* design ideas that the quick instinct to build new gadgets and new products is largely motivated only to embody these technical concepts and "cool" design ideas. No more and no less. The difficulties that the professionals in this industry have with the subjective phenomena, such as the differentiation, appears to be an unfortunate consequence of this instinct. Nevertheless this Gordian knot must be cut.

A proper thinking to create differentiation, on the other hand, differs from the above approach in a crucial way: it turns around and asks the customer the question: "What do these products *mean to you*?" and "What problem are *you* trying to solve?" In substituting this exercise of comparing product attributes with a question aimed squarely at the end user of this product, this proper approach is implicitly *making the end-user an integral part of the differentiation.*

THE MARKETING TRADECRAFT

Let us go back to our finished-product vs. raw materials analogy.

The basic point of this analogy is, the technical design concepts can take on a valid, finished-product form without the need of a human experience. But certain aspects of high technology *execution* function must be drawn into an individual's experience to make sense. These aspects are better understood from *bottom up*.

This bottom-up approach orients one to derive the comprehension from a practical standpoint. When we have this perspective, we always remember how we ourselves have *originally* come to realize a certain execution function. That personal experience never leaves our memory. Now this same memory makes us gravitate towards the habit of *drawing in a customer* into a similar experience, thereby making this customer a part of our value criteria.

A conceptual approach from the top, on the contrary, tries to retrofit the customer to an already formulated feature, in a manner that is fraught with alienating the customer.

Consider the following:

For example one day you and your colleagues would be talking things over at lunch about that morning's meeting with a customer. This customer had an unusual product in mind – at least this is the first time you've ever heard of it – and estimated that with a slight modification to your chip and a support for one or two new external interfaces you could be a contender to be his supplier.

At first you thought, "Well, here's another customer who wants everything customized to him," but then you find yourselves coming back to his idea time and again throughout the day. There was something to his idea, something that seemed *within reach* and the markets he said this product will get you into are most certainly where you want to be in a year or two.

So you and your colleagues sit down at the lunch table and draw up on a piece of paper what exactly this customer wanted, making sure you consult your notes to get it right, on a left side of the paper. Next you ask yourself if you have anything already in the chip specification that can be tweaked into a semblance of this new feature. Finding none you then ask what it takes to build this feature at some point in the near future. First thing you need to know is if your engineering team has anyone that knows how to build this feature.

You keep following this train of thought and pretty soon you have a small chart that you drew on the right side of the paper with names of the designers and system architects you guess would know a thing or two about this new feature. You may not get it exactly right in this back of the envelope approach to figuring out if your technical team has what it takes, but you'd be surprised how close you *do* get to a good estimate.

Without realizing and being aware of it too consciously, you have just reviewed your company in a completely new light – its readiness to enter into a new market – by scrutinizing the talents and skills of your engineering team. Moreover, this exercise seemed almost natural and *essential* for you to figure out if you meet customer's needs. It is only later on when someone tells you that you are actually doing a *skill-gap analysis* you realize, "Oh, is that what it's called?," and leave it at that. The skill-gap analysis is a finished-product. Bu you have arrived at it from a bottom-up approach.

It is this kind of *tradecraft* of execution, amassed from the real-life experience that this book is mostly concerned with.

THE QUESTION STILL REMAINS

So we now know what kind of quality differentiation is. But the question remains: "*What* differentiates one product over another?" *Why* does a customer choose one feature over another, one product over another?

Price, a superior benefit, the timely availability of the product, the opportunity cost, these are all known, measurable metrics. But they don't answer the real question, which still remains unexplored. What is the precisely the root cause, if there is one, behind the customer's *act* of *choosing* one product over another?

In the next chapter we will attempt to explore the answer to the above question.

6

WE RELATE BEFORE
WE DIFFERENTIATE

Take a look around us at any given moment and we notice immediately that we are faced with a striking variety of products in our day-to-day lives.

Our homes and work places are filled with them. From the age old invention such as a bicycle that is parked in our backyards, that color television in our living room and the refrigerator in our kitchen to the cars and power tools in our garages, our daily experience is punctuated with these products.

Not in any ordinary way, but in a quite intimate fashion these products form a thick fabric of the *stuff* through which our very day-to-day creative disposition, what we do at work, the way we define our short-term projects, even our long term goals, are conditioned. So much so that without the humdrum of these products around us, the hours that go by during the day seem so boring and sometimes even depressing.

OUR PROPENSITY TOWARDS ENGINEERED PRODUCTS

What is even more interesting is, whether we are in the middle of an urban setting with all the essential paraphernalia or in the country side answering our inner craving to be far away from the presence of "all this technology," it is a fact that every one of these products is actually built by people: *they are all man-made.*

Someone, somewhere along the way had an idea first, whether driven by a necessity to solve a problem or to act upon one's own creative stimuli. They had then set about on a serious purposive act to build such a product, for example a chisel or a hammer.

Whenever we are faced with a task to perform it is indeed *rare* that we willfully ignore these man-made products around us and go look for a natural object, such as a rock or a log of wood, to do that task. Naturally occurring objects never appeal to us in a way these man-made products do, perhaps because these *built* products represent a basic fulfillment of all our inner urges to advance forward.

In other words, *engineered products* are what we prefer. They are what we are used to. We actually *like* to use them because they are, well, relatively easy to use for the task at hand. We can pick a specific tool for a specific task, whether it is a workshop tool such as a hammer or a wrench, an entertainment device such as a VCR, a DVD player, or an essential workplace device such as a laptop computer or a PDA.

We are surrounded by these engineered products everywhere. That painting or a wall clock that we hang on the wall, the car we drive, the electronic device such as a PDA, the laptop, the bridge we go over to the freeway on-ramp, the fax machine and the phone. It is the same with the semiconductor chips. These chips are used in boxes that do something cool when you turn them on, such as an MP3 player or a video camera.

What separates an engineered product from a natural object? Where does our proclivity towards engineered products come

from? What is its origin? Answers to such questions are the key to
our understanding of the origins of differentiation.

THE QUALITY OF REFERRAL

When you think about it, every engineered product that we see
around us has a specific *use,* a utility, for it. This *quality* of utility is
common to every engineered product that we build. It is a universal
characteristic of everything that exists under the category of
technology. Technology is all about these individual engineered
products which we either use directly, or *as a tool* to make other
engineered products.

For example, engineered products such as a woodworker's fine
chisel, a simple hammer or a drill bit, are employed as tools to make
something else, for example a chair.

On the other hand, we also have instances of devices that we use
directly, as they provide a particular kind of service to us: the chair
we sit on, a high technology gadget such as a PDA device that helps
us organize our personal information.

But there is something more to these engineered products than
their utility. And this is where it gets subtle.

Every engineered product *always refers* to its own utility. This
reference is like a pointer to its stated use. An indication of the
purpose for which the engineered product was originally designed
and built.

When we look at a woodworker's fine chisel we are immediately
reminded of the delicate and exquisite finish of the furniture. The
fine chisel points to the specific action which the skilled wood
engraver performs with this tool. Whatever may be the type of the
engineered product, this *referral quality* is always there. It is like a
we-do-*this*-with-it quality by virtue of which we know where and
how we can use this engineered product.

This quality of *being able to do something specific with it* is
common to every engineered product that we build. Hence, a
hammer immediately brings to mind its purpose of driving in a nail.

This is probably a strange way to think about a product: to speak
in terms of the qualities and references. But remember that this is

exactly how we said we would like to proceed, by peeling off the outer layer of the technology and look at what lies beneath.

So we found this referral quality, but what is so remarkable about it?

ONLY FAMILIAR MEANINGS COUNT

The striking aspect is, regardless of its type, *any engineered product would make sense to us only when it refers to its utility.*

Whatever do we mean by "*only* when it refers to its utility?" Surely an engineered product is not imbued with life so it can scramble and rush to its utility to announce itself whenever it encounters the end user! But something very close is at play here. Let us demonstrate it.

Take the case of the hammer. When we think of this hammer, what comes to our mind? In an instant a series of situations where we can use this hammer flash by in our minds, all of them more or less involving driving in a nail. We can only understand this hammer by looking at what it points to, what it refers to, which is the driving of a nail. You can stare at the hammer all day and not understand what it is, until this driving-a-nail referral hits you and then you go "Aha, that's what this is used for!"

But something else is happening here. Let us turn the above example on its head and ask the question: "What if the hammer *does* refer to its to-drive-in-a-nail utility but *we* still stare at it all day and not understand what this engineered product is?"

But how can this be?

How can we not comprehend this engineered product *as a hammer* when we admit that the hammer does indeed refer to its utility?

This brings us to one of the most important and subtle discoveries in our investigation: the hammer may refer to its utility, but *we* first have to know what this driving-a-nail *means.* In fact, we had to have already known something about driving in a nail for a hammer to make sense to us.

If the notion of driving-a-nail doesn't mean anything to our minds, then we wouldn't be sure what to make of this physical object of the hammer.

The subtlety here is not that a hammer always refers to its utility. But that, for the first time, we are looking into a treasure-chest of all that is *already meaningful* to us, as individuals, and bringing this treasure-chest to bear on what this hammer means to us *now*.

All engineered products have this quality of referral embedded in them in such a way that *only when this referral quality points to something that is already meaningful to us*, would these engineered products start to make sense to us.

How A Product Attains Relevance

Every engineered product points to its purpose: a computer reminds us of the internet access and email, an exercise machine brings to fore a plethora of fitness exercise posture images, a cell phone reminds us of the phone conversations, and while a hammer reminds us of a nail, a nail in turn probably reminds us of a picture that we forgot to hang in our living rooms.

Now imagine a situation in which we are staring at an engineered product and we don't know what this product is. The questions that pop in our mind immediately are usually: "What *is* this strange object?" and "What is it *for*?" because even though we are staring right into it we cannot relate this hitherto-unseen and still-unfamiliar object to anything else that we already know.

A perspective such as this may seem peculiar at first but will soon start to become clear and may even make us wonder why we didn't see this before.

So what did we achieve with this discovery?

It is *of no use to us* to merely know that an engineered product exists. What use was it to simply to know that an engineered product called a "hammer" exists if we couldn't connect it in our minds to the driving-in-a-nail utility? The engineered product must also satisfy the condition that *while* its referral quality is pointing to its own utility, it *must also* refer to something that is already meaningful to *us*.

A RECAP

Let us recapitulate the ground we covered so far: we took a look around us at the day-to-day products we use and realized that these products indeed have a special quality to them. This special quality makes these engineered products always refer to their utility, their purpose.

More important, we discovered that if we cannot comprehend this purpose in terms that we *already know*, then this whole engineered product doesn't really make any sense to us. It does not *mean* anything. Of course when we ask someone to explain to us what this product is, we are simply hoping that this other person would explain it to us in terms that we already know.

All engineered products carry this referral quality embedded in them. In fact it is *always* the case that in all our encounters with the engineered product, this quality of referral is always there, whether we are consciously aware of it or not.

A semiconductor chip such as the popular Pentium processor from Intel Corporation is likewise an engineered product: conceived, designed, built and manufactured by people with the aid of other engineered products. Computers are used to simulate the behavior of the processor design, the expensive fabrication equipment is employed to build the circuits on the silicon, and the testing equipment to test the package.

BACK TO THE INDIVIDUAL DIMENSION

When we explained the engineered product in terms of the above phenomena, what is so special about it?

When we say that an engineered product makes sense to us only if it can be explained in terms which are already familiar to us, what we are really saying is this: any engineered product enters into our awareness only as long as its quality of referral is *always mediated by us*.

In this sense, *we* are the ones who put the engineered product in touch with its purpose. Without us, all engineered products are dangling, disconnected from their purpose.

By uncovering this *innate dependence* of an engineered product on *us*, we have exposed the underbelly of this whole thing called technology and found the secret sauce of successful differentiation.

We shall see how next.

Whenever an individual interacts with an engineered product, the experience that the individual user undergoes *at the moment* of that face-to-face with the engineered product shapes many things. Most prominently, this experience *singularly determines* whether this engineered product has any kind of meaning to this individual or not.

An engineered product, in spite of possessing a physical form, a shape, a feature, a weight and a color to it, cannot rely solely on any of these attributes to attract the attention of the individual user.

So, how does this engineered product attract the attention of the individual user?

Remember what we said: without an individual user, all engineered products are dangling, disconnected from their purpose, waiting for the individual to mediate. At the same time, to be mediated by us, this product must be meaningful to us. In other words, the engineered product's quality of referral has to be a *meaningful* referral quality.

The sole determinant of whether this product makes any sense to the individual user is that meaningful referral quality. The engineered product is at the mercy of that meaningful referral quality. If there is no meaningful referral quality that sparks itself in the individual's mind, then no matter how attractive or colorful this engineered product is, it simply invokes a bewildered stare into it.

A RECAPITULATION

Let us remember that the reason we launched into this investigation is because earlier in the chapter we were stuck with this question: we know differentiation is important, but do we know *why?* How can we understand the underlying reason why a customer chooses one feature over the other?

By now we are starting to see the answer. We now know that simply *describing* an engineered product is not enough (recall the empty and bewildered stares.) The feature-by-feature comparison approach that we alluded to at the beginning of this chapter is nothing but a rich *description* of the product. Not enough.

We then took a next step and learned that only when the referral quality of the engineered product is in such a way that it brings the end user into the picture, that we start to see some action. This is the final proof that an individual user *is and has always been* the essential part of the very idea of an engineered product. Not as an afterthought, but as an essential condition.

We can think of this meaningful referral quality as a switch. An engineered product, with all its embellished bells and whistles comes prancing into view. Nothing happens yet. Now something stirs in the treasure-chest of all that is already meaningful to the individual user. And the switch is turned on. This switch-being-turned-on is a signal to the individual to connect with the engineered product. On the other hand, if the switch remains inactive, all the bells and whistles in the world wouldn't do a thing to make that connection.

Once we grasp this idea of the dependence of the engineered product on the *mediation* by the end user, our worldview changes.

No longer are we justified to look at this world of tools, of gadgets, of instruments and of all the technology products we live in the midst of, as if this world can be all out there bustling with value and a revenue-generating potential *independent* of the end customer's mediation.

We should emphasize that, in speaking this way about the engineered product and its quality of referral, we are not referring to an abstract concept. This referral quality cuts way deeper than that. We relate to everything around us through this meaningful referral quality whenever we handle an engineered product. It is pre-wired into our very mode of existence. Not just the user of this engineered product but everyone who is involved in creating it, marketing and selling it have this kind of relationship with this product.

7

CONTEXTS CAN UNDIFFERENTIATE A PRODUCT!

We have not seen the most interesting part yet.

At the beginning of the book we referred to the underlying layer, that layer which is beneath the technology, as a hotbed of value construction.

From the analysis we just did, we know exactly what this underlying layer appears as. We saw how we ourselves connect to an engineered product by first connecting a *recognizable* purpose to it. As long as we recognize an engineered product in familiar terms, we have no problems connecting with it.

Now that we made that connection to the engineered product, what happens next? How does it lead to a construction of value?

How do we go on to accord one value to a product an entirely different value to another product?

To answer this question, we must now take that all-too important step into the heart of our discussion and develop the notion of a *context*. Let us begin.

A CONTEXT

First, let us step back to the notion of the mediation. That is, the inherent dependence of the engineered product on the ability by the end user to make a connection.

One of the most remarkable aspects of this connection is, we, as people, associate ourselves with these engineered products by way of not one referral but *several* referrals per engineered product.

In our mediation, we don't just connect one purpose, but several purposes to the *same* engineered product.

The most vibrant aspect of this quality of referral is, each time an engineered product evokes a different referral in us, the *meaning* of what this engineered product stands for us at that moment *changes*.

In what way do we connect several purposes to the same engineered product? Surely we don't attribute these multitude of purposes to the same engineered product *simultaneously*, or else there'd be a cacophony of connections and overlapping meanings!

On what basis, then, this meaning of what this engineered product stands for changes?

It all depends upon the *context*.

In one context the hammer might be used to drive in a nail. In another context the same hammer might be a good paper weight on a breezy day while we shuffle the disheveled pages of drawings for a new furniture assembly out in the backyard. We connected with the engineered product hammer by associating it to two different purposes, a tool to drive in a nail and a convenient paper weight, based on a specific context.

Notice that even when we use a hammer as a paper weight, it still possesses that meaningful referral quality, except now it points to the utility of being a paper weight. Nothing changed as far as the engineered product itself. The only change is in the context.

So while the meaningful referral quality belongs (even though changing) to the engineered product, *the context belongs to the subjective world of the individual.*

WE RELATE THROUGH A CONTEXT

Contexts are all about the individual's needs, moods, necessities, goals, evaluations, decisions, just about every aspect that can be called as subjective. Contexts occur in multiplicity because all our experiences are punctuated with a plethora of engineered products and the impressions made by these engineered products in our daily lives.

For a product to have any meaning to us, several factors come together at that moment of time: first there is the context, then there is that meaningful referral quality that draws a connection from the product and joins it with the task in front of us.

A random walk on the bustling and noisy downtown street evokes a million short-lived referrals that rapidly turn anonymous products into a larger pattern of an impression that shapes our likes and dislikes. In fact there are infinite referrals that buzz in the background, most of which we are only fleetingly aware of or even care about. Likewise, a more deliberate and subdued environment such as an inside of an upscale boutique store also has the same effect, only we are more conscious of it, letting favorable referral qualities work their way into our economic choices, whether to buy a certain product or not, and we eventually arrive at these conscious decisions.

This is how we *relate.*

The question lurking here is: "If the utility of the hammer is either to drive in a nail or as a paper weight, then who or what makes us to use a hammer predominantly to drive in a nail?"

The answer lies in the strength of the referral quality. The referral quality of the hammer *as a tool to drive in a nail* is many times stronger than the referral quality of the hammer as a paper weight. Likewise, the referral quality of a real paper weight *as a paper weight* is many times stronger than the referral quality of the hammer as a paper weight.

Of all these contexts in which an engineered product is put to use, there is usually a small set of them that stand out. They stand out by the strength and the dominance of a particular meaningful referral quality that enabled us to perform a certain task most prominently.

We retain a strong association of a particular purpose to the engineered product in our daily lives. How strongly and how consistently we associate a particular purpose to an engineered product depends on the *ease* with which we are able to interact with it in a particular context. It is much easier to use a hammer, than a paper weight, to drive in a nail. So when we think of nails we immediately think of the hammer.

This is how we *differentiate*.

Engineered products that don't demonstrate this strength of purpose don't often penetrate people's contexts in any effective way.

CONTEXT: A CAULDRON OF VALUES

The above example also illustrates a powerful characteristic of contexts: *a context can change, at will, the way an engineered product is put to use without regard to its intended utility when it was originally built.*

The context is the ultimate modulator of how an engineered product is used *as*. This power to efface the intended utility imbues a context with that incessant tendency to *un-differentiate* an engineered product. Surely this ought to be a cause of great concern to technology marketers.

We observed earlier that all decisions we make are made *within a context*. Let us look at an example.

When we think of a personal electronic device such as a cell phone, here the engineered product is the cell phone instrument itself.

We know that the referral quality of the cell phone points to the purpose of the cell phone: to make a phone call. We get stuck in traffic. Not wanting to keep the folks at office waiting for us in a meeting, we pick up our cell phone to make a call. Those few minutes represent a specific context in which this cell phone serves a specific purpose.

At the same time, that cell phone may have a built-in camera. But here in *this* context, this camera has no meaning for us, even though physically it is there right in front of us. This built-in camera then simply has no relevance to us *at this time.* Not because there is anything wrong with the built-in camera feature but because the context is not matched.

On the other hand, any active awareness of the camera that thrusts itself in our mind *while* we are in the phone call context is an intrusion.

If the electronics are built in such a way that forces us to make an adjustment, such as pressing a key or flipping over a keypad for it to switch over from the camera mode to the phone mode, then it is an intrusion.

When such an intrusion happens, it puts in danger the utility of this electronic device in its *entirety* primarily because it lost some of its strength of purpose *as a* cell phone when we needed that strength most in the context of the phone call.

SUBTLE IS THE CONTEXT!

Contexts are very powerful. Not only because they shape the elusive referral qualities of the devices – those elusive forces residing in the mind of the individual – but also because they have a subtle yet a strong impact on the decisions and choices the individual makes.

Whether you are engineering manager planning out your next project, or an end consumer in an electronics store browsing through the latest gadgetry, or a CEO preparing for an upcoming board meeting, contexts unleash their power in subtle ways.

Regardless of what the context is, when you are operating in a mode of actively and with a careful study engage that engineered product into your project, all these referrals, utilities and contexts are working in the back of your mind. They all eventually come together, are filtered, put through a subjective evaluation, stoke a gut feel, bring in a comfort factor, whatever you call it, and finally you come to a decision about this product.

In fact this contextualized way of looking at things can be a helpful framework to understand the world in which a high technology professional operates.

We are about to step into that world in the next chapter.

8

THE SEMICONDUCTOR
COMPANY CONTEXT

So far we have stayed a few feet above the day to day workings in a real high technology company. Let us now delve into the world of a semiconductor company, that ultimate high technology company, where real semiconductor products are built by real people and apply the context framework that we've been developing.

SEMICONDUCTOR CHIP DESIGN CONTEXT

Where does the referral quality come into play in the semiconductor chip design context?

Let us consider the example of a chip product design. Like any object built by an engineered effort, this chip product is also an engineered product.

When the engineering team sets out to build this chip product, there is an initial development phase during which the chip has not *yet* turned into a product.

Nevertheless, in whatever shape and form it is, just like the referral quality of every engineered product, this chip too possesses that referral quality, that something by virtue of which we are drawn towards it.

Within the *context* of the developers who gave birth to it, this chip product carries a rich set of referrals and meanings.

The engineers' intellectual passions that go into building the basic blocks for it, the long hours at night they spend in the laboratory trying to put the pieces together and integrating it into a fully functional live system stand as a testament to these referral qualities. Behind these activities there is a steady humming of the incipient life of the meanings and referrals that only the design engineers can contextualize and relate to.

While at this stage, no doubt that this chip is not a mature product yet, but only exists *as a nascent product.*

But as a nascent product, this chip is already buzzing with a rich array of referral qualities. These referrals engage the minds of the architects and the designers, who are immersed deep in the contexts, and inspire them to infuse the nascent product with the intended functionality and performance.

As a result, the referral quality of the product is also at a nascent stage at this level.

WHERE DOES THE PRODUCT'S UTILITY ORIGINATE?

In other words, at this nascent stage, before the chip evolves into a full product, this referral quality is limited to the purview of the system architects who conceived it, wrote the specs and of the designers who built it.

These designs, the architecture, the specifications, all *point to* the future fact of the chip. It is *for* these individuals, the designers, the architects that this nascent product means what it means.

As the development phase progresses the *fact* of the product starts to take shape. Though at a nascent stage that it may be, this chip is no longer a rock that you stare at all day and not know what to do with it, but is filled with a promise of a fully functional system. This promise is the pointer to a future event.

Where does this pointer come from? Where does it originate?

It originates in the context of the designers, the architects, the programmers, who have all delved into their private contexts, into the referral qualities and the meanings that are in their collective mind. These individuals gave a shape and a structure to all these referral qualities and meanings.

These shapes and structures are manifest in the chip specification, the flow diagram, the system-level model, the testing criteria, the test suite, all of which point to the chip. Through hard work and team effort these individuals eventually manage to convert these already meaningful referral qualities in their collective contexts into a product.

And what does this nascent product do as it starts to take shape into a full-fledged product? *It starts to point back!*

It starts to point back at these very same meanings and referrals which gave rise to its form and shape, these very same meanings and referrals that lie right there in the specifications, in these test suites, and in these system-level models.

This pointing back is like the first signs of recognition by the newborn. When those simulation test results come out, sometimes barely correct, you see them pointing back to the test plan.

Designers and validation engineers never talk about all this in such a fashion but when they see the output of a functional block in the lab just as they expected or formulated it to be if things go right, they definitely feel a connection with the device under the test.

That is when the totality of the chip development product, what with all the scrambling to go to work early morning and staying late, starts to form itself into a bigger context that has a bigger meaning and a larger referral quality to it. This totality is by virtue of the pointing back nature of the constantly evolving product.

And that's not even the most important aspect of it.

The most important result of this process is: *whatever pointing back this nascent product does at these initial stages, it becomes final the referral quality for the product when the nascent product turns into a full-fledged product.*

In other words, what determines the final referral quality of the product when it is completed is nothing but these initial pointing back and forth amongst the initial contexts, meanings, and the referrals that are in the collective mind of the engineers and the designers.

Whether this nascent product eventually turns out to be just a rock that you stare at all day and not know what to do with it, or if it vibrates with multitudes of referrals in the end-user context depends on this initial interplay.

FROM A DESIGN TO A PRODUCT

How does this nascent product find its place from the engineering laboratory to the external world?

Now we have come to the crux of what we are building this whole framework up to. We are going to ask the question, "What makes a product be a success when it travels out from the designer's laboratory to the external world of the customer? What is it that infuses this engineered product with that unique quality that makes the customer want to buy it?"

For this we once again turn to the central point of referrals, meanings and contexts.

As long as the product is in the laboratory, the *source* of its referral quality lies in the collective contexts of the designers, the system architects and engineers. It is through the contexts of the technical documents, system diagrams, the test plans, the standards specifications, that the nascent product gains its referral quality by the act of the pointing back to these contexts. The designer finds the nascent product meaningful by virtue of this referral quality.

Most importantly, as long as the referral quality is derived *solely* from the laboratory contexts, this quality will enable the nascent product to live *only* within these contexts. This referral quality will prove insufficient for this engineered product to sustain itself outside of the laboratory context.

How, then, does the nascent product evolve into a full-fledged product?

If the referral quality that breathed the signs of life to this nascent product is not enough to help evolve this nascent product into a full-fledged product, then is this nascent product doomed to die and be castaway the moment it steps into the external world?

To avoid such a premature demise, as the nascent product shifts its environment from the laboratory to the external world of the customer, *the nascent product must support the contexts and multiple referrals that are unique to this external world of the customer.* Only then this nascent product will be able to evolve into a full-fledged product.

But how can it be possible? How can this product, which was baked and built within the confines of the laboratory and development environment of the designer, how can we expect it to refer to anything meaningful in the external world of customer?

In fact, how can this product be of any meaning to *anyone* other than the designers who built it?

These questions bring us to the central point in our discussion, the missing piece of the puzzle.

THE BASIS FOR A MARKETING FUNCTION

The engineered product can sustain in the external world only when the meaning and the measure of the utility of this product, *is derived from those contexts that belong to the subjective world of the customer.*

It is these customer contexts that are the source of the infusion of the lifeblood for this product's sustenance in the external world. For the product to possess this quality of being able to evoke referrals in the customer's mind, to be of any meaning to the customer, *the product must point back at the customer's contexts!*

But so far these customer contexts have been sitting out there on the other side, not really having anything to do with the formation of this engineered product. There must exist a mechanism or a function that links and connects these customer contexts back *to* the formative stages of this engineered product so that when the product is brought into the external world of the customer, the customer starts to feel that "Aha, this is how I use it. Makes perfect sense to me!" moment instead of just a rock that you stare at all day and not know what to do with it. And this function that makes these links and connections is the *marketing function.*

Throughout the course of a product conception, the definition, the design, the building of it and subsequent delivery to the customer, it is the marketing function that is responsible to elicit those particulars from the multiple contexts of the customer and translate them into *features* for the product.

When you have a feature in a product with a clear benefit to the customer, the product automatically starts to point back at the customer's multiple contexts, evoking a rich set of possibilities and potentials for the customer when he makes use of this product.

The essence of marketing lies in transplanting this engineered product that the designers, the architects built in the laboratory, and bring it *into* the customer's world.

This transplantation is a movement of the engineered product *from* within the confines that is wholly and tightly coupled to one context – the context of the system architects, the designers, and the development environment – *into* the customer's context, in such a manner that the engineered product takes on the vibrancy and life in the contexts of the customer's world.

When the marketing function is successful in doing that, then the company deserves to be paid by the customer.

Imagine you are an observer and you are watching your customer cast his glance at your product. Then imagine that no matter how hard the customer tries, he cannot escape this feeling of staring at a rock for long time as it still doesn't ring any strong bells in his mind.

If it is so, then it is not because there is anything wrong physically or electronically with the product. It is simply because you have not extracted those particulars from the customer's context and transplanted them into the formative contexts of the product, *prior* to the product completion.

Had you transplanted these customer context particulars into product features, then these particulars would have immediately evoked strong referral qualities in customer's mind.

PART 2

THE FORWARD MOVEMENT LATENT
IN EXECUTION

9

A GLIMPSE AT THE
MARKETING CONTEXT

A remarkable aspect of semiconductor companies is how seemingly out of character the marketing role can appear when compared to the rest of the goings-on in the company.

Predominantly driven by the innovations that take place in the *technology* space, the semiconductor chip sector is distinctly characterized by the *tangible* nature of its products. We can see and touch the chips. All of us more or less know that somewhere behind that tightly screwed-in back cover of our cell phones, the laptops, the smart phones etc., is a set of integrated circuits that do the magic tricks. We are emphatic in asserting that these chips are an embodiment of the *technology*, not of the marketing. Even the logo of the company displayed on the chip – the ultimate manifestation of a marketing activity – immediately brings to our mind images of sharp, brilliant engineers sitting at these companies and engaged in esoteric *technical* design activities that seem so, well, *complicated.*

Even within the confines of the chip companies, leaving aside the broader impression at the industry sector-level, this apparent anonymous nature of the marketing function is dominant. In the eyes of a design engineer, there is a mystifying element to the job that the marketing guy across the hallway does. Perhaps it is because the *measurability* that is at the core of the design activity is nearly invisible in the marketing activity.

To an engineer, no matter how complicated a chip design project is, it is always possible to break down the progress of the project in terms of measurable milestones. Individual sub-system design modules can be quantified in terms of the silicon space, the power consumption, the cost, the money and the effort it takes to build such a module, a crisply defined interface between a module and its neighbors. Finally, there is that clear and a deterministic description of the actual function this module performs within the overall system. Everything is so *factual.*

But nothing like this exists in marketing. Well, nearly.

When it comes to a genuine grasp of the role of the marketing group, rarely such a thing exists in an engineering group. What is prominently visible is a whole lot of buzz. In a typical engineer's mind, a marketer is largely a self-aggrandizing figure and an unwanted intrusion in design review meetings. There are few sights more awkward and embarrassing than watching a technically incompetent marketer engaged in a technical argument with his engineering counterpart.

Most engineering designers believe that semiconductor marketers are simply those engineers who couldn't make it in the intellectually superior world of design. The *causal connection,* from what a marketer does to the actual results, is invisible. In fact it is even unclear what the actual results are.

Nevertheless, every thing that a chip marketer does is as specific, as goal oriented and as measurable as anything else. The perspectives developed in preceding chapters are an attempt to provide a thinking person's basis for placing the marketing function in the high technology corporation. The purpose of this chapter is to clear away some of that cloud surrounding the marketing role and draw that causal connection between the marketing activity and the success of the company.

Let us first look at the qualitative aspect of this connection.

MARKETING IS KNOWING THE PROBLEM

At the outset, a semiconductor marketer's primary job is to move as much product as possible from within the confines of the company (also called factory in the semiconductor industry parlance) to the customer in a profitable manner.

A Marketer Moves The Product From Company to Customer

If you are a marketer, what would you do to accomplish this goal?

First, you can *create* a compelling demand for your product in customer's mind so that customer buys from you. Apple Computer's iPod™ is a great example.

Second, you can fulfill an already created demand, perhaps created by you or by your competitor at an earlier time or by an external market and regulatory forces. Or, you can simply increase the number of customers that demand your product that you are shipping already.

No matter what approach is employed, across the spectrum from the above-mentioned simple techniques to highly sophisticated marketing strategies, all good semiconductor marketing *first and foremost excels in clearly articulating a problem* that is big enough that the solution is worth a premium, and second, *crafts a compelling product as a solution to that problem.*

ROCK SOLID FOCUS

A state of the art semiconductor chip takes at least two to three revisions (also referred to as re-spins) of tapeout before it is fully made clear of the bugs and is qualified to be market-ready. It takes anywhere from eight to sixteen months from the conception stage to the first spin of the chip, and thereafter four to five months per additional re-spin. Rarely do chips assume full functionality right after the first spin.

As a result, on an average it takes two full years for a chip company from the chip idea stage to be able to place production-worthy chip samples in customer hands. In the meantime the world moves on, competitors gain prominence, and a few customers may go out of business. New paradigms emerge in the market making the chip product obsolete or premature even before it is complete (witness the premature demise of broadband wireless in the late 1990s and subsequent signs of resurgence beginning in the early 2004.)

Throughout such a turbulence, which has become more or less the norm in the electronics industry these days, the responsibility of semiconductor marketing is to maintain a *rock solid focus* on the goal that the company has set out to reach, which is to achieve a working product as early as it can.

MARKETING AS AN ANCHOR

If the chip company is a startup with limited marketing personnel, then quite often there is a real danger that the development effort can become detached from the external customer. As a consequence of this detachment, the chip so designed can turn out to fall short of the customer's requirements, let alone meet his high expectations. Which is when there is a distinct possibility that the hunkered down efforts from the design team to get to the finish line can only result in a disappointment. This can happen and often does happen in the semiconductor startup world.

On the other hand, if the product arrives from the fab in a working condition, and qualified ready to be shipped, then this success only means one thing: that the whole cycle must be repeated once again for the next generation chip product.

There is a threefold implication to our above observations.

First, the marketing function is the key to the chip company *throughout* the beginning-to-the-end process of the chip development, the design wins, subsequent market penetration and expansion.

Second, the chip marketing's role does not stop with one product. This process is a never-ending one throughout the life cycle of the company. Moreover, it only becomes more complex with each product's success. Without the marketing's leadership role in each such turn of the cycle, the company can degenerate and throw away its successes.

Third, the *organization* of the semiconductor marketing function closely follow the chronological phases of the company evolution, starting with the chip product development followed by the market development and expansion. For example, at the beginning stages as the core team is being built and the company is bracing for an exciting product development phase, the departments such as sales, marketing communication, PR tend to have a low key role. As the technology and product development nears completion, marketing becomes an increasingly essential function to secure the customers and design wins.

TECHNOLOGY IS DIGITAL, BUT MARKETING IS ANALOG

A cursory glance at the "Corporate Profile" page of any semiconductor company website reveals a fairly customary partitioning of the responsibilities among its management team. Product definition, promotion, sales and distribution belong to the marketing and sales realm.

Although the job descriptions don't articulate it *in this particular manner*, it is helpful to look at the big-picture view of the marketing function in the following way:

THE DRIFT

When we set aside the mind-boggling complexity of the technology that goes into making the chip, take away the seemingly out of the world technical nature of the semiconductor industry value chain, and strip down the company to its basic economic model, it is just *that*, an economic entity and a business that must make money.

If you are a CEO of this company, you need someone *on your side* to tell you what product to build. To this end you need an interface with the customer.

Then you have to make sure that your development team is indeed building exactly that right product and *not something else*.

And once this product is built, you need someone else to ensure that this product goes out to the customer in a timely manner.

In as much as we would like to believe that the people that we hire in our companies to take up these responsibilities would hold steady, like anything in our real and analog world, *drift* happens. The threat of a passive abandonment to the external market forces is always lurking.

In addition, there are at least two unseen forces that are constantly at play that can, and more often will, destabilize this economic business entity. They are the *threat of anonymity* and a *lack of identity*.

THE THREAT OF ANONYMITY

The biggest barrier that a company faces from the beginning of its inception is the *threat of anonymity*.

Put yourselves in the shoes of your CEO and you'll have a feel for how many things that require simultaneous attention.

Everything from knowing what to build, who could potentially be your customer, where can you get pertinent information about your markets, how do you find people that know this stuff, where do you find these people, how you can verify that the information you working with is the right one, the list goes on.

All of this has a strong tendency to remain anonymous to you. Why? Largely because as an economic entity your company hasn't yet acquired the required contours and borders to identify itself in the marketplace. And until that happens, by strong, willful, passionate and focused efforts by the people in the company, the market place subjects everything and everyone into this anonymity.

LACK OF IDENTITY

Third, is the *persistent lack of identity.*

As you start to become visible to your customers and your partners, to your aghast you will simultaneously discover that you are not alone in your market place. Seemingly suddenly and out of nowhere you have competition! Not only that, but your competitor's actions have a tendency to throw you back into the anonymity from which you emerged through all that hard work.

Marketing is all about fighting these unseen yet deadly forces of drift, anonymity and lack of identity.

In many ways when you look at the structure of the marketing organization the semiconductor world, there is an underlying partitioning, a division of labor, to attack these threatening forces. At the same time, it is not like these forces show up at the door, knock and announce which one it is so that the right marketing personnel is sent to the fore to ward away the enemy.

As a result, the marketing roles and responsibilities, while clearly defined in terms of the ownership, tend to be somewhat fluid and change from company to company. Startups with no product yet, companies with the first product ready to go to market, large companies with multiple product lines, and lastly the industry leaders, all have their own subtleties in the way they organize and perform semiconductor marketing.

Let us take a broad sweep at these roles for a qualitative view.

PRODUCT MANAGEMENT

This marketing function is responsible for everything that has anything to do with the *product* directly. That includes defining what the product is, knowing what the company needs to bring it to a reality and identifying those customers who can make use of this product in an economic way.

Product marketing, which is often a sub-function of product management, sometimes is the name under which these functions are performed in smaller companies where you may not see anyone with the "product management" in the job title. As the company gets bigger, product marketing tends to morph itself into the "outbound marketing" role while the product management and planning function takes over the "inbound" facing priorities.

STRATEGIC MARKETING

Semiconductor companies must do strategic marketing because the market forces of the drift, the threat of anonymity and lack of identity don't come with a blueprint of how to maneuver them.

Strategic marketing, at the heart of it, is the willingness, the ability and the performance of the company to analyze these forces, identify and grasp crucial customer problems lying behind these turbulent forces *and* to propose a plan to solve these problems.

When the chip company is convinced that it has the right plan and executes on this plan, the overall effect is that these turbulences will temporarily calm down, allowing the company to be prominently seen by its customers for what it does, i.e., solve the customer's problems.

CUSTOMER MARKETING

Once a customer is engaged, all the interaction with this customer pertaining to the product, other than the interactions on the technical support and other than the detailed technical design reviews, are handled by customer marketing.

As in everything else discussed in this book, it is important to remember that the various events and issues, whether of the business, financial, operational, or of the tactical nature, unravel over *a span of time.* This span may range from the day-to-day, the near term of weeks, the short term of the quarterly and the longer term of the fiscal year to year.

Keeping this *temporal dimension* in mind is important to appreciate the conditions in which the chip company has to operate. For example, keeping the customer informed with the release schedule during the various stages in the chip product, to instill a sense of confidence in customer's mind about your company's execution capability.

Every communication with the customer, as we have talked extensively elsewhere in the book, is a management of the *expectation*. A big part of the customer marketing is the expectations management. If there is a delay in the product development schedule, then simply sending an intimation to the customer of this schedule change will only prompt this customer to start looking elsewhere for the chip supply.

Product schedule delays are always deleterious to the chip company. When such delays occur, there is an immediate and sometimes irreparable damage of the trust in the eyes of the customer. The customer marketing function ensures that such a *mere intimation* never takes place. Instead, the customer marketing owns this expectations management task and communicates this message to the customer in a way that minimizes the loss of face to the customer and still retains their trust and their business.

PR AND MARKETING COMMUNICATIONS

If the product management and strategic marketing functions are mainly focused on getting the right information *into* the company for making the right decisions on the product, the marketing communications (or "marcom" in the industry parlance) and public relations manages its dual counterpart.

They are responsible for the complementary role of making the company be known in the industry community and to let everyone know of the company's existence and identity. They make sure the right information and the right image of the company is flowing *into the industry*. This group accomplishes this objective by building collateral whose content, the tone and the delivery are specifically aimed to project a particular message about the company. In this sense, this group is instrumental in overcoming the force of persistent lack of identity that we referred to above.

THE SPARK NEGLECTED WILL BURN THE HOUSE

A remarkable aspect of working with a startup is that infectious spark that the whole experience seems to evoke in an individual. To an aspiring startup company team, there is probably nothing more important than to maintain this slow burning spark. It constantly fires up the embers of inspiration among the technology development team.

But this same spark when neglected has a negative potential, to paraphrase Tolstoy, to burn the house. This negative characteristic arises ever-so surreptitiously in the friction between marketing and engineering groups.

How can a company detect the signs of this neglect? What are the tell-tale signs?

To an informed mind, these signs are easy to detect. When individuals in engineering and marketing groups become too engrossed in their own context, visible symptoms start to appear. By their very nature, the marketing and engineering contexts are distinctly different. It is up to the individuals, whose responsibility it is to perform these functions, to look beyond their own context.

For example, to an engineer, when compared to the logical, deterministic and mathematically sound world of electronic systems design, the intangible, a highly dynamic and a largely formula-less discipline of marketing seems like a seat-of-the-pants approach.

As a result, to most engineers, marketing is by and large nothing more than a general-purpose function for the industry analysis, best relegated to the periphery, away from the core activities of real product design.

With a few exceptions, this is how "the house burns." When these context-limited views become the prevalent culture in the technology-driven firms, the damage is already done.

THE TASK AT HAND

A direct consequence of this culture is a peculiar kind of friction between marketers and engineers that is dominant in these companies. Peculiar because this friction among the rank-and-file is tolerated, taken for granted and even leveraged to conduct intra-company political warfare by the mid-level managers and senior executives.

In all the literature on high tech corporate leadership, management and marketing, the subject of the interaction between marketers and engineers is the least covered. Although there is a loud acknowledgment that it is perhaps the most challenging aspect of any high tech corporate leadership, the near-universal friction between marketing and engineering teams is considered nothing more than a "people management" issue, and is often dealt by the mid-level management only as an afterthought.

There's even a mythical belief that this friction is a *necessary* evil.

In an effort to dispel that myth, we have developed the context framework. As it is, our context framework has already made us aware of notions such as the opportunity cost, the economic value, the idea of differentiation, etc., the notions that drive the marketing discipline, *any* marketing discipline.

In other words, this framework allowed us to demonstrate that the key lies in clear and simple explanation of the underlying economic principles that drive the marketing function in a high technology company.

Rather than simply accepting the text-book notions of these economic principles, we *re-constructed these notions anew*, except that this renewal is based *in the context* of the marketing function.

In the next chapter we continue our renewed way of looking at the high technology profession and examine one of most vibrant contexts in a high technology company: *the execution context.*

10

THE CONTEXT OF EXECUTION

We are now ready to apply our context framework to that often-found culprit behind a company failure: *the ad hoc and context-less execution.*

Let us start with the question, "What is the execution context?"

To execute simply means to put into motion a set of tasks according to a prior plan. So we have two separate entities at play here: a prior plan, a strategy, and the subsequent execution of it.

Nevertheless, such clean separation into a plan first, then action next, is not often feasible in real world high technology corporations. Markets move too fast for companies to luxuriate in the planning that is disconnected from active execution. In this sense, strictly speaking, everything is execution, including formulating a plan.

No doubt there is plenty of literature on the high-level corporate strategy. Books, business journals and the industry press are abound with discussions on marketing techniques for branding, on product positioning and so on under the rubric of high technology marketing.

Nevertheless, these expositions by and large assume that a *market-ready product exists* and then proceed to talk about business leadership. And when the question of the product does arise, it is framed more often as an engineering matter, and relegated to the project or program management discipline.

Of course both the business leadership and the engineering excellence are indeed the foundations for any company. But these two derive almost exclusively and so much from their own disciplines that they have become too cloistered. Imagine if the primary colors become too unwieldy to be blended with one another. What use, then, would these colors be for a painter's pallet?

A successful execution of either a business or a technology strategy in a high technology company requires exactly that, a blended approach where the people who execute do so with the *correct balance of contexts*.

For example, look at how most semiconductor companies, especially the startups, execute on a day-to-day basis. Most rely on the recollections and experiences of the individual employees. It is an *ad hoc* approach wrapped inside a homespun process. While engineers develop the technology, they have little or no visibility into that aspect of marketing which deals exclusively with *turning a design idea into a market-ready product. This is because the company has no execution context.*

It doesn't have to be that way.

THE DISCIPLINE OF EXECUTION

Starting with this chapter we begin to apply the context framework as a *practical* tool.

We will attempt to establish the foundations of execution discipline in a high technology company by creating an execution context. In doing so we are not as much interested in a blanket criticism of existing business practices, some of which actually work quite well, nor are we interested in prescribing one more new process.

On the contrary, our aim is to bring about a renewal of a particular kind of mindset, a particular kind of thinking that so often accompanies a successful high technology company but that which has not been communicated widely.

Although our discussion centers on a semiconductor company, the thinking elicited here goes to the heart of nearly every high technology company.

So what is the discipline of execution in a semiconductor company? What is the mindset that a successful semiconductor industry professional works with, on a day-to-day basis? How should a semiconductor professional approach this discipline of execution?

We begin by first introducing the most fundamental tenet of the semiconductor business, what we call *the circle of execution*.

THE CIRCLE OF EXECUTION

The most important action a semiconductor marketer must perform in order to be successful is actually a three-fold function:

1. Get the right product definition
2. Achieve a design win
3. Deliver the product *in time*

There it is. It is that simple.

Everything else that a marketer does are secondary. Attending seminars, delivering speeches, giving talks at industry conferences and tradeshows with slick product and corporate presentations, getting oneself quoted in the industry press, all these matter only after the circle of execution is firmly held in control.

Walking into a semiconductor company, a marketer immediately becomes accountable for these three concrete and strongly intertwined responsibilities.

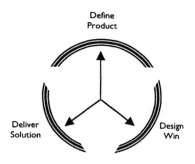

The Circle of Execution

Every time a chip company plans a new product, these three objectives must be fulfilled. Taken together, these three actions constitute what a company must do, to bring the product into the market successfully. They constitute the specific *execution* steps. The company must score a win on all three counts to be successful.

By its very definition, it is immediately clear that an essential aspect of the circle of execution is its never-ending *cyclical* nature.

A product is defined first, the development gets under way and a customer design win is secured. As soon as a working sample of the current product is delivered to the customers, the definition of the *next* product is already underway and the cycle repeats. In the meantime, the volume production of the current product starts to ramp up.

In this manner, the three hands on the dial are always turning to stay synchronized with the changing customer needs and market conditions.

EXECUTION IS NOT A BUSINESS PROCESS

Many startups falter at the very first step of getting the product definition right and not realize it until they find themselves spinning wheels in the quicksand of disappearing beta customers and sinking chances of a design win with it. Scores of others may actually define the product right but fail to execute on the all-too important step of making the product to work early enough for the customer.

One reason for the engineering-marketing friction is, the teams are not prepared to tackle the pressures imposed by the circle of execution. This lack of readiness to move with the changing market conditions almost entirely causes the disharmony between the engineering and marketing teams.

Add to this the proclivity of most semiconductor marketers to fuel the confusion, by secluding the big picture view of their thinking to the engineers. Senior management invests considerable time and effort to craft detailed strategy playbooks which, by design, only coordinated marketing and engineering groups can execute.

But so often it happens that, while engineers develop technology, they have little or no visibility into this circle of execution.

How does this circle of execution manifest in terms of the timelines? What happens *first*?

A snapshot of single-iteration in the circle of execution necessarily involves a complete sequence of events in a product's life cycle. These events create a genesis for the product, bring the product to reality, fulfill the product's business purpose by selling it in sufficient volumes to generate the expected revenue, before it is put to rest by the next generation product.

But there is more to the process than these sequence of events.

Each event is a specific activity *performed by individuals* in the company. *This is not a business process that can be automated.* As we shall see, each event is actually decision boundary.

A Corporation As a Confluence of Contexts

Remember what we earlier said of the contexts.

Within the scope of this chip company, the day-to-day busy-ness is filled with the contexts of the individuals, namely all the employees of the company, who play a part in it. Every single action they undertake has a direct impact on shaping the overall context. More important, their disposition towards the task-at-hand, i.e., their own sense of urgency and their sense of priorities, is what really governs how they do it.

From this context framework viewpoint, a company itself is a big context, consisting of a host of mini sub-contexts, popping up and disappearing almost on a daily basis, with the decisions as trigger points.

So if every employee brings their own worldview to the party, shaped by their own pasts contexts, past experiences, then what guarantees that these worldviews don't conflict and seize the company into a standstill?

Looking at the way we described the contexts, the worldviews with their infinite varieties, it seems a pell-mell and a recipe for disorder. It appears as if this approach of ours provides no toehold. Are we at a dead-end?

On the contrary, the answer is right in front of our eyes.

It is indeed true that a company with no explicit sense of direction will be subject to the uncontrollable forces of individual worldviews and subjective contexts. Fault-lines open up where they didn't exist before, creating communication gaps, expectations gaps among the rank and file. In this mode, the fate of the company is a tossup.

What we need is an equalizing force, a *common context* in which the referral qualities, the utilities and the purposes are same for every employee.

Where is that common context? How shall we orient ourselves to look at it, if it is hidden?

Actually, we are already closer to the answer than it appears.

We have already seen in the previous chapter that there is a semiconductor company context that qualifies this requirement. *It is made up of at least two distinct contexts: a developer's context and a customer's context.*

The nascent product is first born in the developer's, i.e., the technological context. Then, as the customer's context starts to appear on the horizon, this nascent product then evolves into a full-fledged product.

There is, in addition, a *third* context without which the corporate entity cannot sustain itself in the free market enterprise.

This is the *economic* context.

We have now arrived at a framework of contexts for a high technology corporation. We state it as follows: *For a high technology company to thrive, these three larger contexts, i.e., the technological, the customer and the economic, must drive whatever the individual employees create, build and deploy in the market.*

Every execution activity that happens in the company falls in one or more of these three contexts. From this holistic point of view, a high technology company is simply a confluence of the three contexts.

The Three Contexts That Makeup A Company

But, *how* does this confluence take place? What are the *practical ways* in which these contexts and their confluence manifest in the company?

Furthermore, how is the circle of execution connected to the three contexts?

EXECUTION AS A FORWARD MOVEMENT IN CONTEXTS

We are now ready to answer that question.

The context framework equips us with a powerful paradigm to connect the three contexts with the circle of execution. We make this connection in three statements below.

First, the circle of execution is nothing but the fundamental force that transforms the company from *one context to another context, in a forward movement.*

Second, each actionable element of the circle of execution, i.e., the product definition, the design win and the delivery on time, is an action that is to be viewed for what it really is, *a choice and a decision making act.*

Finally, no such choice and decision making act occurs in isolation. Instead, every execution action must be situated within the three contexts of the technological, the customer and the economic.

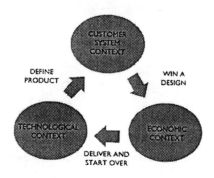

Execution Manifests in Forward Movement Between Contexts

The high technology company's success lies in organizing itself around this forward movement dynamic between the execution contexts.

EXAMPLE

As an example, let's take the case of the product definition.

A glimpse at the execution action, at the mindset involved in the new product definition, reveals that this entire process can be traced back to the technological, the overall customer system and the economic contexts.

Every activity that is concerned with the system design on the chip has a strong technical nature to it, and belongs to the technological context. It is clear right away that the people at the center of this context are engineering groups. Their concern is filled with the chip specifications, the design and development environment, the standards documents that drive the minimum performance requirements, the test environment that they construct in the laboratory and so on.

On the other hand, as soon as the marketing and sales force starts to engage an external customer prospect, another context starts to take shape: the overall customer system context.

In this context, the concern is not so much *directly* about the design of the chip, but with the *system* environment, with the box in which this chip is a primary component. The people at the center of this context are the prospective customers, the marketing and sales and the application support engineers. In fact, in many ways the company employs these individuals for the sole purpose of building the overall system context.

It is in this overall customer system context that the reference board and system requirements originate. At the same time, the nature of the overall customer system also changes from one segment to another. In fact, *even within the given segment the overall customer system changes from one customer to another customer!* That is because each customer deliberately makes it so, in order to differentiate their system from their competitors.

Finally the economic context brings it all home.

The *value* of the chip changes from one customer segment to another. This difference in value leads to an opportunity to set the pricing of the chip differently in these segments.

The economic context is where the business case for the product is made. This is also where the choices and the decisions on the direction of the business unit are made. Several activities fall into this category. The volume and revenue projections, the consideration of the risk factors, the market and economic conditions, the pricing strategies, alignment with the customer roadmaps, all these are brought together in the economic context.

THE TAKEAWAY

When properly understood, contexts will have a decisive effect in the execution. No doubt one executes a plan, not a context. But what the individual brings to the execution, the ability to grasp what is important and what is not, the leadership qualities without explicitly being too self-conscious of them, all these intangible skills are brewed in the three contexts.

No matter how the titles of the individuals are carved out in the organization, at the end of the day what matters is how well the company creates the execution context and executes on the circle of execution.

A context plays a powerful role in shaping what engineered products *mean*. Right from the beginning, from the cocoon-to-chrysalis evolution, all the way through the shaping of the utility in how an engineered product is put to use, the contexts rule.

In the end, the takeaway is this. The product starts its origin in the technological context, within the confines of the technical specification and the laboratory. It must then evolve not only into the customer system context, but eventually into the economic context in order for the company to execute on the roadmap.

Remember that the meaning of an engineered product changes with the context. This meaning-changing effect is strongly at play in the context-framework of the company. One should know the contexts because each context changes the meaning of the product. The same product that appears one way in the technological context, takes on a different meaning in the overall customer system context and a still more variation in the economic context.

Engineers and marketers have different views of the product because their native contexts are not the same. These native contexts provide them with different sense of their place in the company.

In a company where the execution context has not yet set in, their professional training drives them so deeply into their own contexts as to make the confluence of these contexts nearly impossible. This is when the dysfunctional culture starts to set in.

What is the role of marketing in creating the forward movement? How should we understand what marketers do as a forward movement creating activity? This is the topic of the next section.

MARKETING INTERFACES EVERYTHING

In many ways, if you are an engineer turning to a position in high technology marketing – especially a position with "product marketing" in its title – you will, in a matter of a few days, realize that this role forces you to discover aspects of the business that you never really thought were handled by people.

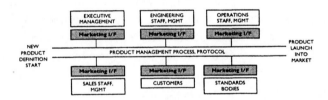

Marketing Interfaces Everything in a Company

Until now, you thought things just happened naturally because, well, because you and tens of others like you showed up at work everyday. Somehow the very presence of so many intelligent and highly educated people at work has the effect of things getting done.

But now you will discover that not only *anything and everything that happens in the company* is driven by a *human decision*, but everything happens because it is actually done by a specific individual with a specific goal in mind.

The reason why it all becomes clear as soon as you get closer to a marketing role is simply because the marketing function is the glue that binds these activities together. In every step of the circle of execution, the marketing function leads the way.

Nevertheless, there is nothing that says that these functions should be limited to the marketing group. The context framework teaches us that the forward movement cuts across the artificial boundaries of the engineering and marketing groups.

Of course in practical terms it makes every sense to carve out the responsibilities among these groups. We are not recommending any overhaul to the structure of the organization. We are here referring to the mindset. The forward movement inherent in execution must be activated across all functional groups, in order to create the execution context.

CONTEXTS VS. DECISION MAKING

How should we think for making a decision? In the company context, it is not only important to be able to make the right decision, but also to know *how the other party* is making their decisions. If you are a product manager, you are always trying to understand what criteria is important to your engineering manager and your customer. The opportunity cost illustration presented earlier in the book is all about trying to get to know *how* your customer decides.

Knowing *how* someone arrives at a decision is as much a key to success as it is to know *what* that decision ultimately is going to be. When we make this shift in the emphasis, from merely interested in knowing *what* those decisions are, to a desire to understand the criteria behind the decision-making process, we are stepping into the realm of contexts.

Contexts, as we saw in the previous sections, are building blocks of a fundamental nature. What they are *not*, are a *technique* that we can choose to ignore or apply at will. A context is not a concept.

On the contrary, contexts belong to the subjective world of an individual. Contexts make the same engineered product appear in a different light. This power of contexts is so extensive that how an individual user makes decisions depends not so much on the physical or electronic embodiment of the engineered product itself, but depends on what the product *means* to him.

When we relate to a certain entity in a certain way, we are *already* making up our mind on what we might do with it. In other words, our context has already driven our minds to assume a decisive stance. By the same reason, to understand how someone makes a decision, we must start at the very beginning, starting from getting to know what their context is and *how* they relate to the engineered product in this context.

Contexts influence how we relate to the products, what we create and build in such a manner that in everything we *do*, they bring to bear the sum of all our experiences until that moment, into that action. The technological context that we saw earlier is one such example of this influence.

As that context in which a product is initially conceived and built, the technological context determines the life of the product from then on. This technological context must be instilled early on with the necessary life-sustaining features from the customer's context. Someone must deliberately, consciously and methodically perform this careful infusion. By casting the marketing function with this responsibility, we at once arrived at where we want to be: the day-to-day grounded reality of a chip company.

CONTEXTS VS. EXPERIENCE

Contexts are nothing if not the very constituents of an individual's experience. Whenever we compare one individual with another and speak of one's superior professional experience over the other, our impressions and judgments are based are contexts, even though we may not explicitly think that way.

We are convinced that the genuinely experienced individuals are really so, by virtue of a vast treasury of contexts they amassed in their experience and their *contextual* decision making skills. Their ability to intuitively articulate a product *as* befitting either a technological context, an economic context, or a customer context is a strength we come to rely on.

We already saw in the previous chapter how a context wields its power over the making of a chip product. We should note that this context-oriented manner of looking at things should not really be all that new. Contexts are not an artifact of a new technology, nor have they started showing up overnight because of a certain turn in the modern technology.

We have always dealt with the engineered products around us in this manner. It is just that historically, in the initial stages of modern electronics, during the early 1970s, because everything was so new, any referral quality an engineered product had, *it* became the dominant one.

Moreover, people who used these engineered products tended to be those who are themselves technologists. The contexts of technologists were relatively well defined and unchanging.

Not anymore. As the technology itself has become more pervasive, and as more and more people, millions more, have made the engineered products an integral part of their day-to-day lives, the very fabric of human experience is now punctuated with these contexts.

What does it tell us? It tells us that any effort at the improvement in the execution success of a company should have to start at this context level. Our thinking, right from the beginning, would have to get used to the idea that for a product to be successful in the market we should think contexts first, then products.

A BASIC SCHEMA FOR EXECUTION

Let us return to the execution context. So we said that an execution context is when the circle of execution confluences with the three fundamental contexts in a forward movement. How can one make use of this notion *in practice*?

For this, we turn to the block-oriented thinking we discussed earlier in the book.

From the execution context viewpoint, each block is no longer a mere set of tasks with inputs and outputs, but *is a context unto itself*. Each stage has a decision threshold. Decisions are to be made within a context that transforms it to the next context. The forward movement is triggered when the decision threshold is crossed and thus the company moves forward.

As a high technology professional, every time we find ourselves with a task-at-hand, the execution context framework suggests the following manner of looking at it:

First, reframe the situation we are in *as a context*.

A Basic Schema for Execution

Next, we must continuously probe the context to figure out the explicit, tangible, human-driven actions required to create the forward movement. As we know that different things mean differently to others based on their contexts, a big part of our task is to get a sense of this same situation in terms of these other contexts.

Everything that happens in a context really starts with these two basic tenets. Let us now summarize the basic schema of execution in the following manner:

1. High technology execution is a series of interrelated actions, in which each action is set in a context.
2. We should know the contexts and actions in such a way that, for every action we should define and identify a context.
3. Next, ask the question, "What are the decisions and the decision thresholds that bring about the forward movement?"
4. By making the right decisions we, as individuals, provide the necessary mediation that eventually results in this forward movement.
5. We should know the context in terms of its *specifics*. And know the individuals involved. Not just their titles and roles but their names and a way to communicate with them. These individuals may be customers, or the engineers, sales managers, support staff, or marketing personnel from your own company.
6. Know for yourself the requisite actions in specific terms. What information *you* need to perform these actions?
7. Know the deliverables, again in specific terms.

8. Know the pitfalls. Do you *know* what happens if you do not do this?

UNFURLING THE EXECUTION CONTEXTS

Now that we have formulated a basic schema for the execution, it is now time to express the whole of the execution *in terms of this schema.*

In the beginning of the book we insisted that, to derive an insight of any value from our investigation, one must delve into the specifics of the context. A high-level, qualitative, conceptual prescription would simply not do. More so because we are dealing here with the subjective phenomena of individual decision making skills, execution actions and experience, and not with a technical concept.

In keeping with our original insistence, in the next few chapters we will unfold the details of the three contexts, as they appear in a semiconductor company, and how they come in interplay with the execution actions.

In these ensuing chapters, we will break down the circle of execution into the individual schema of execution, and identify the forward movement causing factors.

We will start by making a minor detour and take a macro-level sweep of the semiconductor value chain so as to gain a big-picture view of *how business is done* in this industry.

PART 3

HIGH TECH CONTEXTS: A SEMICONDUCTOR COMPANY VIEW

12

THE
SEMICONDUCTOR
VALUE CHAIN

A good way to understand the business of semiconductors is to take a step back, and look at a big picture of the *value chain*. In this chapter we will take an example electronics product and look at how this products traverses through the value chain and eventually gets to market. To this end, let us consider a product whose popularity is on the rise, a wireless LAN router, WLAN router for short.

When a consumer such as you and me is looking to install a wireless internet connection at our homes, we typically have two alternatives. We either call up a broadband service provider (for example, here in Silicon Valley, California we would call SBC or

Earthlink for DSL or a Comcast or AT&T for Cable Modem service) and have them send us a box with installation instructions.

Alternately, we could walk into a nearest electronics store and buy the box ourselves, making sure we pick the right one from among a myriad of choices we see on the store shelves.

Either way, with that act of purchasing this box, we, as an end consumer, have fulfilled the eager expectations of a multi-billion dollar semiconductor industry. A proper understanding of semiconductor business and marketing starts from here.

WHO SELLS TO WHOM

Consider the box that we just bought. The name on the box, indicating the company that manufactures it is referred as an OEM, for Original Equipment Manufacturer. The OEM is also called a "box maker" because this wireless internet router product is boxed in a ready-to-use form by the OEM.

How did that wireless WLAN router box get to the electronics store?

It got there because the folks at the store had *purchased* it from the OEM either directly or through a distributor. A slew of business criteria had been taken into account before the store made the decision to stock its shelves with this WLAN router product. That includes the price they are charged by the seller (OEM), and the amount of shelf-space available in the store.

Most importantly, the store also considers the price which it thinks it can charge to attract the end consumer such as you and me so that we continue to go to *this* electronics store, instead of to a rival store.

Among the decision makers at this electronics store are the product marketing and sales people strategizing on how to exert their influence over the OEM to extract the best price that they can get.

Remember, the price that the electronics store pays for every box of the WLAN router to the OEM (the supplier) is a *cost* to it. The store will then add its own markup to this unit cost and that becomes a price tag for you and me.

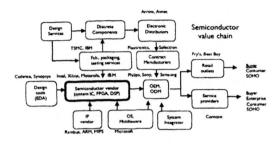

The Semiconductor Value Chain

The point of this example is to emphasize a fundamental fact that drives the engine of the semiconductor business, *any* business for that matter. That is, when boxes and goods move from one pit-stop to another pit-stop up and down the value chain, as from an OEM to a retail electronics store in this example, it is *always* via the action of selling and buying. Though obvious this point may seem, it is often lost in the vagueness with which we all suffer, when it comes to thinking about the markets. It is neither through an act of courtesy nor as a favor to the store owner that this wireless router is on the store shelf. There are significant forces of market at play behind this seemingly simple appearance of the box on the shelf.

Not only that, the seller (the OEM) who makes a profitable sale is the glad to have made this sale and *walks away with that profit*. The buyer (the retail store) of this inventory now assumes the risk and responsibility of having to sell this inventory in turn to the next pit-stop in the value chain – in this case you and me – with a high expectation of a profit.

OEM

Simply put, an OEM is a business entity that is interested mainly in knowing what products and gadgets the end consumers can be convinced to buy. It will then *build* these products. Notice the immediate difference between a retail outlet such as the electronics store and an OEM. The retail store does not build anything. Instead it just *buys* the product from an OEM, turns around and sells it to the end consumer.

The next step in our investigation is to look at how this WLAN router product takes on the shape that it has at the OEM pit-stop. As such this box is put together by assembling its components, so let us look at who the suppliers are for the OEM.

The WLAN router box is equipped with foldable antennas that are stretched upright when the box is on. When we connect the power cable, the front-panel lights up with blinking LED lights. The plastic casing itself has air vent holes, impact protection at the corners, on the sides, at the top and bottom. A plethora of connectors are built into the backside of this box, including the connection for the power cord. This is just the outside of the box.

THE BILL OF MATERIALS

An inside look into the box reveals the electronics, including the semiconductor chips, all placed on a small printed circuit board.

An OEM is not that much interested in building just *any* product. Instead, it focuses on building a product that is in some way uniquely appealing to the end consumer. To this end, each and every part that we see inside and outside of the WLAN router box is scrutinized thoroughly to meet this requirement.

A cursory look at what we are able to do with this box gives us an idea of the complexity involved in the design and the validation of the box.

In addition to doing what it says it does – to let us access internet securely at high speed without requiring any wires – a consumer must be able to use this box with any broadband service provider (given that the type of the box matches with the type of broadband service i.e., a WLAN router for a DSL broadband service and a WLAN cable modem for a broadband cable modem service.) In addition, if the box is sold through the service provider, then the service provider needs remote access to the box. This is to manage the user authentication, security, troubleshooting and various day-to-day management functions, without any interruption in the service. These functionalities are typically provided by means of a special category of software called *middleware*.

In a nutshell, a considerable investment of the OEM's time, resources and the development cost goes into integrating together a combination of software, the hardware, the semiconductor chips, and the supporting electronics components into a highly functional box that the WLAN router is.

Although an OEM builds the products that a retail outlet sells to the end consumer, not all the components that go into building this box are built by the OEM itself. Instead, an OEM will direct a majority of its focus on knowing, and gathering from the market, exactly *what* kind of a product is in the next wave of attraction for the consumer.

An OEM does this by employing a dedicated sales and marketing force whose job it is to stay engaged with their buyers, the retail outlets and service providers. These sales and marketing personnel gather the *requirements* that these retailers and service providers continuously develop through their interaction with the end consumers such as you and me.

Armed with this knowledge of *what to build*, an OEM will focus its in-house development primarily on integrating those components that it buys from its suppliers.

One such component that is unique, and which enables the OEM's box product to standout from the crowd, is the semiconductor chip.

In fact the semiconductor chips are usually the first in the line of components that an OEM investigates. A semiconductor chip is an integral part of all the planning that goes into an OEM's product development. The product design and engineering groups in OEM companies meticulously maintain a detailed list of all the components that make up the end product. This list is referred as a bill-of-materials, or a BOM for short.

CONTRACT MANUFACTURER

Next in the economic value chain of semiconductor industry is a contract manufacturer.

To understand precisely why a contract manufacturer exists, we must take a step back and distinguish between the *design* and the *manufacturing* aspects of a product development.

In the semiconductor value chain there is a special place for whoever conceives the idea, converts that idea into a design and owns the intellectual property rights to the design. That entity commands a significantly larger premium from the market compared to someone who only manufactures this product. So these entities, typically semiconductor chip makers and OEM box makers, increasingly divert their resources into the research and design, leaving the manufacturing to the contract manufacturer.

A contract manufacturer builds the products that the OEM designs and owns the rights to. A contract manufacturer is not all that interested in whose name it is on the label of the product. A contract manufacturer typically executes the behind-the-scenes tasks of manufacturing the product with a high degree of quality and ensuring that the product is certified by the various certification bodies across the world.

Another important aspect to remember as we traverse up and down the value chain is that not all companies in the value chain make products that are usable by the end consumer. For example, an end consumer has no use for the semiconductor chips by themselves.

BACK TO SEMICONDUCTORS

Semiconductor marketing is concerned with making sure that the design, development, and manufacturing of these semiconductor chips is done in such a way that fulfills the OEM's requirements.

While the overall goal of a semiconductor company is to secure high-volume orders from an OEM customer for its chips, the focus of the semiconductor marketing personnel is on *knowing* every requirement from the OEM upfront.

With this brief interlude behind us, let us now go back to the execution context discussion.

13

THE PRODUCT DEFINITION CONTEXT

We are now in the thick of things. What we did until now, in the previous chapters, is a sort of clearing the way. We familiarized ourselves with a few essential elements of *how to think* like a good semiconductor marketer.

In the ensuing chapters we are going step into the practical realm. We will take each element in the circle of execution i.e., the product definition, the design win, the timely product delivery, and introduce ourselves to how they are executed by people in real semiconductor companies.

Note that we are not interested in what the right approach to execution should be. We are not ready to make such prescriptions yet. Our goal is to understand how the circle of execution comes together with the three semiconductor company contexts, the technological, the customer and the economic.

It is that confluence, where the execution actions are seen not in isolation, but soaked in the contexts, that is at the heart of our renewed thinking.

These chapters are intended to serve as an essential introduction, not just to the technology professionals, but to anyone inquisitive, of *how products are crafted and brought to market.*

WHAT PRODUCT

Earlier we talked about the reorientation of the product. What we meant by that is, to be useful in the company's product portfolio, we must bring economic value into the utility of the product. Only then the reorientation of the product occurs.

That is the product a company can make use of. A technology-centric product that is reoriented to an economic value generating product. The product's value grows from that of the technological to that of the economical *only* when we infuse customer's preferred features into the engineer's context.

We often hear the words "product requirements." When we say these two words, we are really referring to a two-fold question.

First, "What is that product?"

Second, assuming we know what that product is, "What are the requirements for that product to be competitive?"

Knowing what a product is and defining competitive requirements for it are two *separate,* but not independent, activities. The contexts that drive these two actions have subtle differences.

Let us first ask the question with this emphasis: "*What* product?"

To answer this question a whole host of factors come into play. The vision of the company, the strategy to get there, the roadmap that supports this strategy and the line of products that enable the company progress from one point on the roadmap to the next point, each step closer to realizing the vision.

A serious investment of the chip company's marketing resources into developing the product requirements makes sense only *after* the company decides what products to build.

THE BIG WHEEL OF ECONOMY AND MARKETS

Let us take a step back and contextualize a product, *any* product. For this we turn to a macro view of the economy and markets.

Products are born out of a peculiar kind of a friction, between a company's insatiable *desire for forward movement* on one hand and on the other, the opportunities created by another company's forward movement. This is the big wheel of the free-market based economy, always turning, creating, morphing, destroying and recreating contexts, values and products.

At the center of this wheel is the product as defined by its requirements. At the outer edge the forces of the turn are the economy and the turbulence in the markets that have a direct bearing on the product at any given time. For example the consumer electronics market is characterized by the volatile pricing power – the ability of the sellers to dictate higher prices for their products - and most semiconductor chip companies are directly affected by this volatility.

This is another facet of what ails the engineering groups in a high technology company. The often seen malaise of the failure to execute in semiconductor chip companies can be traced back to the *manner* in which this wheel is comprehended.

Engineering organizations often oversimplify the dynamic nature of the market and assume that the wheel is static and standing still. Rarely, if ever, has that been the case in the semiconductor markets. The requirements for the product are almost never cast in stone. The reality is, this wheel is turning incessantly. As a consequence, the requirements for the product are always subject to the pressure to change and adapt.

Once we get past these macro-level changes imposed by the economy and by the markets, there are other factors that influence the chip product definition.

In general, the nature of how we define chip products depend to a certain extent on the *type* of the semiconductor product, namely whether the chip is an ASIC, an ASSP or a programmable chip such as an FPGA or a DSP (including reconfigurable processors.)

In fact, what is also important is to remember that each type of product definition demands subtle changes in the *thinking* because these product type variations actually result from the differences in the types of the *customer* in each case.

For example, if your product is semiconductor IP (intellectual property), then your customer is a system-on-chip semiconductor manufacturer, but if your product is a finished semiconductor device, as in an ASIC, an FPGA or a DSP processor, then your customer is an OEM (original equipment manufacturer.) These two types of customers have distinctly different overall customer system contexts.

DEMAND

How *does* a company decide what products to build? It depends on the size of the company and how long it has been around.

If it is a new *startup*, the answer is quite often simple: the founders of the company already had an idea to begin with. They build on this idea and that leads to a certain kind of the product. These ideas come from the founders' careful observations of the goings-on in the high-tech world of products and the *demand* for these products in the business and consumer markets.

But, wait a minute, aren't we being circular? If new product ideas come from the market demand, then doesn't it imply that the market already *knows* the product it wants?

Yes of course, in a way. A market has no way of demanding a product that it doesn't already know that it wants. But how exactly does a demand phenomena happen? How do markets know *in the first place* what product to demand?

We will not attempt to answer this hugely complicated question in its entirety but will say this. It is useful to think of the demand in high-tech markets as a sort of a *trailing* phenomenon, trailing behind something else that comes first. What appears first is a certain kind of widespread belief that this product *solves a problem*. When enough people, who experience the same problem, believe that this product solves that problem, or mitigates the problem in a significant way, that belief itself gathers momentum and assumes an economic dimension of its own. When the same people are willing to act on this belief and put down their money to buy this product, we have the makings of the demand.

The curious nature of the markets is, most of what is visible to us, the stories we read in the newspapers, the product reviews in the trade press, the gadgets and appliances we see on the shelves of the electronics and appliance stores, *all of this is similarly a trailing phenomenon.* All these products are here on the shelves because something, a chain of events, happened before, *before* these products came to be on these shelves.

These controlled chains of events are triggered by a flow of behavior, such as the end-consumers' buying patterns, which in turn triggered groups of people in various participant companies up and down the semiconductor value chain. Some of these people in the value chain may never be in contact with each other, but it prompts them to scramble in a strange sort of synchronous timeline, aiming for that elusive time-to-market window, culminating in all these shelves being stocked with *these* products and not some *other* products. We describe the specifics of this value chain in the earlier chapter on the semiconductor value chain.

In the case of a more mature semiconductor company, its products are already in market, generating revenue and profitability. The thinking in such a mature company on what products to build involves a wider perspective on the *vision* of the company. It involves the ideas that look beyond the day-to-day camaraderie, and beyond the tangible nature of the here-and-now product portfolio. It aims for a larger role of the company in the macro-economy of the region and calls for the kind of the motivations and inspirations to which the employees respond in a *personal* way. Once again, the marketing function is largely responsible to craft this vision and point the way for the CEO to lead.

ROADMAP: A BLUEPRINT FOR FORWARD MOVEMENT

Large semiconductor companies typically have product portfolios that span multiple market segments. It is quite typical of these large semiconductor companies (for example, Intel Corporation) to have hundreds of products in their portfolio. Most are already deployed in the market and generating revenue, several others ready to be launched and quite a few in the formative stages of the definition, design and manufacture.

These products are managed by the market segment-specific groups in the company, organized along business lines or business units. While the vision for the overall company is formulated at the highest levels of the executive management, the task of crafting a strategy, the *means* to follow the path that is being shown by this vision, is quite often tightly coupled to the specific market segments and hence left to these business units.

Rooted firmly in the vision for the company, the key individuals of these business units lay out a path that shows what they plan to do between now and, say the next two years, to ensure that the company is following the path as shown by the vision.

This plan is often a result of several days-long closed door *strategy* discussions among the business unit executives. It shows a series of product recommendations laid out on a year-by-year or a quarter-by-quarter timescale, called the *roadmap*.

The roadmap is, at its core, a blueprint for the company's future plans and hence is guarded with utmost secrecy. Effective roadmaps communicate clearly. If we put our finger on one point on the roadmap timescale and ask this question first, "What are one or two key *problems* that if solved, would generate an attractive *demand* for the product that solves them?" The roadmap then recommends that *that* product be built at that time on the scale.

Remember we said earlier that the demand is usually a trailing effect which follows when a product solves a problem. If the business unit *executes* successfully, i.e., develops the right product and delivers the product in a timely manner to the customer in a way that fulfills the revenue expectations, then the revenue generated from this demand would propel the company *forward*. The business unit then gets to execute the *next* product on the roadmap by asking the same question, "What problem can we solve here which propels us forward to the next competitive product?"

There is a cyclical nature to this, combined with *a forward movement*: find a problem, build a product that solves that problem, find another problem, build *that* product and so on. Individuals who are adept at recognizing the contexts they are in are the key to bring about this forward movement.

It is not a coincidence that this cycle ties in exactly to that other cycle, i.e., the circle of execution: define the product, design a win and deliver the solution.

The organization within the business unit is structured with the aim of running this unit as a small company in itself, with its own profit and loss statements. The challenges in ensuring that this product planning takes on a realistic and competitive form revolve around the coordination of marketing, engineering and sales. As the business unit converges on the roadmap that is in line with the strategy and the vision of the company, it becomes imperative that these three groups wholeheartedly buy into the roadmap.

THE PRODUCT LINE

In large semiconductor companies with products already in the market, decisions on what products to build and on the specifics of the roadmap are more likely to be based on the products that already present in that *product line*.

The term product line is typically referred to that group of products, that subset of the complete product portfolio which serves a specific segment of the market.

For example, the market segment of wireless communication might be broken down into short-range wireless such as WLAN and long-range wireless such as cellular. A WLAN product line would be the one that consists of products specifically made for the WLAN market, with variations on products each with a different application. Similarly a cellular communications line of products.

Regardless of how a company chooses to splice these definitions, the existing line of products usually form the baseline for a new product definition. This is because these existing products indicate the kinds of intellectual property the company already has, or is currently being developed on another project, and the skill sets the engineering teams acquired during these past projects. These existing products also have a history of the *relationships* these groups have built over a course of time with the suppliers and, most importantly, the customers in these market segments.

Moreover, the marketing and engineering teams themselves have had a chance to work together in these past projects. They have forged relationships among one another and smoothened them out so this gives the management a chance to pick the winning teams. These relationships *among and between* the product line managers, the product marketing managers, the system architects, the business unit managers, the designers, the sales managers, the account managers etc., form the bedrock throughout the new product's definition, creation, subsequent deployment in the market profitably.

THE ESSENTIAL SKEW IN A CORPORATION

A question that every company poses to itself and encourages all management personnel in its business units to think about is, "How do we choose *what products* we should build so that our business grows to be the number one or number two in our markets?"

One of the vexing management problems that beset technology-driven companies is how little the rank and file think about this question. As such the question posed above is really a corporate *goal* and requires a solid understanding of the nature of the problem itself in terms of how to get there.

The search for the products that propel the company into high ranking places necessarily includes two essential requirements:

First, a product that both solves a customer problem and has a clear place in the company's overall strategy.

Second, a compelling *business* case that justifies that such a product is worth building.

As a matter of fact, the original question, "How do we choose what products we should build so that our business grows to be the number one or number two in our markets?" itself requires that the coil springs wound into the new product should unwind in *two equally important contexts*: the customer context and the economic context.

It should be made clear at the outset that the end goal of a product company is *not* just the excellence in research and technology. On the contrary, although every company no doubt should strive to be excellent in the research and technology, the end goal is the two-fold imperative of solving a customer's problem and realizing a compelling business case.

This is no different from how a baseball game is decided: regardless of how well the pitcher does (the technology imperative) the team that wins is the team that scores more runs (the business imperative.) At the same time, it is also true that regardless of how many runs the team scores (business team), if the pitching staff (technology team) is less than excellent, there is every chance that the team loses.

In this sense, there is an asymmetrical relationship that is *skewed* towards the economic value generation for the survival and growth of the company. Between the technology behind the product and the business ahead of the product, this asymmetry is skewed *towards* the business end of the product. Companies and the employees that do not grasp this essential truth are often the first victims of the execution malaise that we warn repeatedly in this book.

THE PRODUCT REVIEW BOARD

A general practice in chip companies to manage this new product definition phase is through a *product review board* (PRB.) Essentially this is a panel that reviews the recommendations of marketing and engineering teams on what products to build.

As the strategy discussions converge on the roadmap, it is up to the engineering managers and the product managers to define the product in detail. The PRB looks toward the marketing and the engineering managers to identify and craft the product. The PRB's expectation is to ensure that the product is defined in such a way that it not only meets the criteria set by the roadmap but also satisfies the two essential requirements described above.

Then, armed with the clear knowledge of the business unit's profitability goals, the panel either approves the recommendation or sends them back to do some more work until they get it right. The PRB is typically headed by the business unit manager, who has the P & L (profit and loss) responsibility. The PRB plays an important role in acting as a decision-making authority. Its panel includes representatives from all sides, and the decision-making process is meant to ensure that it involves all these sides.

It is quite normal for this joint preparation of PRB presentation to be stretched over a few weeks' duration. At the end of this period, the respective managers from the marketing and the engineering groups – the *joint owners* of this product – appear in front of the panel of the PRB to pitch their case.

At this stage, the expectation of the PRB is that most of the major kinks in the product definition have been smoothed out and there is an overall agreement between the marketing and the engineering.

From marketing standpoint, the product's definition has been baked enough, the schedule reflects the expectations of when the product can be available to the customer and the business case is attractive.

From the engineering point of view the proper resources have been identified and assigned. There is sufficient flexibility factored into the schedule to meet the delivery deadlines and a reasonable overall budget estimate is made which is then used to make the business case.

The PRB panel then grills these managers extensively to ascertain the robustness of the business case and goes over every detail of the material presented with a fine tooth comb.

Keep in mind that the future of the business unit for the next 12 to 16 months depends on the decision the panel makes here at this PRB session. If the business case so presented passes this thorough scrutiny, then the PRB approves the project, kicking off a long and a risk-laden process of the new product development.

This is, in a nutshell, more or less the *process* followed – a sort of a *what* happens - during the new product definition phase in a typical large semiconductor company.

IN CONCLUSION

So there it is. The context space for the product definition.

By its very nature a context, *any* context, cannot be grasped in all its specificities. There are infinite variations of how individuals face their roles and responsibilities, although the corporate umbrella bounds these variations by streamlining the "best practice" processes. Nevertheless, we hope this *approach* presents the reader with an upfront comprehension of how the execution action of product definition is done in real high technology companies.

At the beginning of this book we referred to the idea of the opportunity cost as a *pre-decision* event in the mind of the consumer. Recall that we contrasted this opportunity cost with the conventional view of the budgetary cost, which is clearly a *post-decision cost*. The fact is, with the engineering manager, the choice is already made and hence the cost becomes a fixed, physical concept that must be managed.

On the other hand, with the customer, the choice is never really already made, but only considered. And there are always alternatives available to the customer. Having made the choice to develop a product, the company is committed and hence has to deal with problem of managing the cost, whereas the customer, with an enviable position of having a plethora of choices, is merely involved.

In this sense, at one end of the spectrum, where the consumer resides, it is full of choices. At the other end of the spectrum is the producer, the chip maker. Within the four walls of this chip company there is a rigid, objective world of budgetary planning and management. Here the cost is stripped of its choice attribute in the sense that the company has *already made a choice* to build that product on its roadmap.

This fundamental diversity, the inescapable difference in the situations of an engineering manager within the closed confines of the product engineering environment and of the marketing manager in the opportunity-cost laden market environment, strikes at the root of almost every conceivable interaction between marketing and engineering.

In the next chapter we will focus on the context space for building the business case for the new product.

14

THE ECONOMICS
CONTEXT

Now we are crossing the boundary of one context and stepping into another. We are entering into the realm of the business case.

The same engineered product, which appeared in one way in the product definition context, is going to take on a different context here. As a consequence, the meaning of this product, how it is interpreted, is also going to change. The language differs too. People in this new context are not going to bother themselves with how the product is defined, nor are they overly interested in what the superior features of this product are.

What exactly *is* a business case? Simply put, it is a demonstration in terms of quantitative figures that for every dollar the company is going to put into developing this product, it is going to get more in return, perhaps two or three times, at a known future time, and in a predictable way. Every aspect of this demonstration is important: how much more is the return, how long it takes to generate this return and how predictable and assured this return is.

So a business case is an argument that tries to prove the claims of the stated return on the investment (ROI.) It is important to note that in making a case for a new product, or for that matter even for an entirely new start-up, the business case is simply a projection *forward* into the future.

Business cases are merely convictions wrapped up in presentations and documents, at least until the time the profitability becomes real in the financial statements. For the individual who authors it, a business case is the conviction that there is this world in the future, which you can see from the here and now, for which you and only you hold the keys. If you do everything that you laid out in this business case document, you get to open the door and find that pot of gold called ROI behind that door.

Knowing fully well this speculative nature of the business case argument, the PRB panel usually zeroes in on the essentials rather quickly. In the thorough scrutiny of any business case one skips all these stage-setting arguments for value proposition, market differentiation, how cool the technology is, and glances at that ROI figure and that brings it all home.

A BUSINESS CASE IS SIMPLY A CONVICTION

When we look at the business case for what it is, several facets come to light immediately. First, it looks a lot like the opportunity cost, because lurking behind both these ideas is a same casting forward nature, this future expectation of the benefit.

If you are presenting the business case to the business unit manager who has the P&L responsibility, the crux of your argument goes like this. In reality your project is only *one* of the several avenues available for the business unit manager to invest his money and commitment. Nevertheless your project is the only one that minimizes the business unit manager's opportunity cost.

Second, the specific day-to-day activities in building the business case for a new product are strewn with assumptions. This in itself is not a bad thing, if only they are taken for what they are, *assumptions* that need to be proven by executing against them. Nevertheless, it is not always true that everyone understands this and acts accordingly.

To see what we mean, take one such assumption for example, that a customer X is likely to place a significantly high volume order for this product four or five quarters from now.

For some unknown reason, as the engineering project gets underway, there is a slow but sure transformation in how this assumption is perceived in the minds of the product teams. The likelihood assumption *changes* into a working conception of a *surety!* And this change happens based absolutely on no additional information!

It is as if the mere passage of time and that one sees over and over again a huge volume order number next to this customer X in presentations during staff review meetings, seem to have a mesmerizing effect. The team is drawn into believing that it is only a matter of time before they see those big dollars start to come in.

And in that false belief, the engineering team makes an automatic leap of faith from a mere likelihood that requires hard work to bring into a reality, to the reality waiting to happen and it's just a matter of time. So much so that when a request for the modification of a feature here or a feature there shows up at the door, the stance taken by the engineering groups is often complacent, drawn from this false belief of an assured customer.

THE THINKING IN BUSINESS CASE

Let's take a closer look at the assumptions we referred earlier that abound a business case. The logic in the business case, in the context of a new semiconductor product definition, is quite straightforward.

Here is how the business case financials are built in a real semiconductor company.

You first pull together all the cost estimates, the design, development and manufacturing costs in making this product. Next you make an estimate of how many units of this chip you think you can realistically sell over a given period of time. This period of time can be three or four quarters after the product is available or the entire life of the product.

Whatever the period may be, the goal is to show that at the end of this period, the revenues in *actual* dollars you are able to generate from selling these chips will exceed all the combined costs of making this chip. In other words, the goals is to demonstrate the ROI, the return on investment.

As innocuous and straightforward as this approach seems, a business case actually requires that several important questions must be answered thoroughly.

For example, how does one make an estimate of how many chips the company *can* sell? At what price are we going to sell these chips? Who or what determines this price? Is the price the same for every customer?

Just the breakdown of the various costs - the design, the development and the manufacturing - itself will involve numerous details of interconnected dependencies that vary with the product features. In each case, these dependencies must be isolated, and their individual costs quantitatively estimated before a reasonable estimate of the overall cost can be made.

Also, it is a matter of great importance how your customer base looks like. Are they a small number of them, say two or three, who will place large volume orders? When you combine these orders, is it sufficient to hit your revenue targets? Or are they a several number of them each of which may place only small to medium volume orders? Here you need many more of these orders to make up for your revenue targets. And what is the minimum revenue dollars the business unit needs to see *relative* to all the costs, before the management starts to feel comfortable about the whole project? Margins are probably number one concern for business management.

It's All About The Numbers

The construction of the business case requires a methodical approach to specifically answering questions such as these.

Where hard data are not available, reasonable assumptions are made. That means that we have to make the best possible assumption, with the quantitative data to back up this assumption. In this manner you build one assumption on top of the other with a strong justification and backup numbers behind each assumption so that it supports the arguments for the next stage.

In a classic ASIC chip case, the product is for a small set of known OEM customers. The customer will tell you that they need this product and if you build it they will buy X amount of volumes. Here the decision of whether to engage in this business and start building the product involves an assessment of the risk. The chip company will, and must, ensure that this OEM customer is financially sound before proceeding with the product development. This is because once the chip is built, no other OEM customer can make use of it because it was specifically customized for this OEM customer.

No matter what the product may be, the business case for a new chip project must demonstrate its strength in terms of quantitative numbers. Here it is all about the numbers and what story they tell. *Qualitative* observations about the market trends are important too, but they serve the purpose better if articulated as the interpretations of the charts and the tables representing this quantitative data.

To understand how this process works, let's look at a somewhat simplistic illustration.

The revenue generated by a chip product is related to the volumes of units shipped, in the straightforward equation as shown below:

Revenue in dollars = (volumes of units shipped) x (price in dollars per unit)

The amount of business that the plan says can be generated from this product is expressed in the business case in terms of the above three quantities. Basically the essence of the business case can be summed up as a justification, a reasoning, for the above quantitative numbers.

Imagine that you are tasked to build a business case. How would you proceed?

Let's look at the first term on the right hand side: *volumes of units shipped*, i.e., the number of chips actually shipped to the customer.

REVENUE PROJECTION

Where does a number such as this come from? What does it look like? A straightforward way to get a feel for this number is to look at your customer prospect list.

Take the top ten prospects from this customer list and make a realistic estimation of what volumes they will purchase for the next three to four quarters. Add them up and you will have a preliminary figure of how much you can expect to ship. Keep in mind that at this stage this number is at best your realistic, *subjective* projection. It is based solely on your, or your sales force's, personal interaction with these ten customer prospects.

More important, this estimation is based on an *assumption* that your product will be ready to be shipped to the customer by a certain month of the quarter.

Now onto the second term on the right hand side of the above equation: *price in dollars per unit.*

What about the price per unit? A simplistic estimate of the chip price, also called the average selling price (ASP), can be arrived at from what you have learned from customer conversations. In your day-to-day interaction with the customer prospect, you are always on the alert for a new piece of information, however innocuous it may seem. Also a ball park price of a comparable chip from your competitors is a good indicator of where the market is going and what price it can support.

Once again, the ASP projection must take into account the time of availability of your chip. In a rapidly growing market it is normal to see a degradation in the price that your customers are willing to pay for your chip. Quite often these price degradations happen because your OEM customer is subject to similar price degrading forces on *his* product (the end product box). There is a tremendous pressure on the OEM customer to reduce the component costs and as far as that goes, your chip is just another component in OEM's box.

As straightforward as the above portrayal of the revenue projection seems, it is also quite simplistic, just enough to keep the product definition process moving forward.

A more realistic approach would be mindful of the divergent nature of the market. The reality is, among those ten different customer prospects in your list, not all of them are building the same box. Hence not all of them have the same need.

For example, if you are building a semiconductor chip for a WLAN protocol, then the end user applications that are made possible by your chip can be quite varied: a high-speed internet access network within a consumer home, or a corporate-wide enterprise network with heavy emphasis on the security of the network, or a consumer device such as a set-top-box with audio and video streaming features. Regardless of what these specific end applications are, the OEM customers have different problems that they are looking to solve with the aid of your chip product so that those solutions will gain them entry into these markets.

SEGMENTING FOR REVENUE

A realistic approach to projecting the volumes that you can expect to ship starts by *segmenting* the customer prospects in terms of these end markets. As you begin to distinguish each segment and lay out the defining characteristics of that segment, a *segment-specific context* begins to emerge.

Recall that in our discussion of the product's path from a technological context to the economic value context, it has to pass through the intermediate overall customer system context. The segment-specific context is closer to the overall customer system context. Even though the technology behind your chip product remains the same across all these segments, when you look at the overall system context in each of these segments, they all look different. In fact not only the overall customer system context, but the respective economic contexts are also different in each of these end markets.

Hence, the economic value of your product in each of these segments is markedly different. This difference in the economic value sets the stage for the chip company to *set the price for the chip* in a manner that is consistent with the economic value in each of these segments.

In other words, the pricing of the *same* chip can be, and mostly is, different from one segment to another.

So now we can rewrite the above simplistic revenue equation in the following modified manner:

Revenue in dollars = [segment A volumes x chip price in segment A] + [segment B volumes x chip price in segment B] + [segment B volumes x chip price in segment C]

As a consequence, the business case task is now broken down into subtasks of developing strong assumptions and backup data for each of these segments. Finally, the customers that make up these segments must be identified.

Also keep in mind that customer's roadmap does not move with your roadmap. What this means is, your revenue projections are only good to the month or the quarter by which your chip must be ready to be shipped to the customer. What happens to these revenue projections in case of a slip in schedule is a whole another exercise that marketing teams often have to quantify.

BOTTOM UP VS. TOP DOWN

So far we arrived at these projections in a *bottom-up* approach – projections from actual customer prospects summed up to a top-level volume number – coupled with a economic-value driven price for each segment.

Once a set of revenue projections are on hand, it becomes imperative that these projection numbers be verified – "sanity check" in the industry parlance – by taking an alternative, *top-down* approach.

In a top down approach, also called market trends approach, you look at these market segments from an outside-in point of view, setting aside your chip product for the purposes of this exercise.

From a macro perspective, you ask questions such as why a certain market segment is growing. Are there any regulatory barriers that have just come down? For example, a hot frequency band in the radio frequency spectrum that just became free. What consumer patterns are developing that are catalysts for this market's growth? For example, the rapid increase in world wide internet usage, and most new laptop computers being equipped with wireless internet access feature.

In this top down market research approach your primary sources of information are the market analysts and their research report.

THE COST CONTEXT

By far we have only touched on the revenue side of the business case. Recall that the making of the business case involves cost side of the equation as well. After all, a business case demonstrates that the revenues in *actual* dollars the company can conceivably generate from selling these chips will exceed all the combined costs of making the chip.

Now let's turn our attention to the *cost* side of the equation.

Before we get into the cost context, let us review how the semiconductor chips come to exist in the market.

HOW CHIPS ARE BUILT

Semiconductor chips are designed *once* and manufactured (fabricated) *many times*. There is a long upfront development phase in which a complete system that is to be implemented on the chip is conceived, researched, and designed.

All the technical details are captured in the form of block diagrams, developed on black and white boards in engineering conference rooms, and in designers' notes during the design phase.

These block diagrams are then written out into algorithms, captured into the EDA and other high-level system design tools. They are then simulated on high-speed computers for various functional and timing verifications, and finally a set of electronic files are generated containing the layout of the electronic circuitry of the complete system.

These layout files are like the printer's block for the complete system, except this printer's block for the chip is immensely complex in its layout. Millions of silicon transistors are arranged in a specific manner and interconnected with still more millions of thin wires that run all over the length and breadth of this printer's block.

Once such layout files are generated, the design phase is deemed complete. These electronic files are then sent over from the chip company to the chip fabrication plant (chip is then "taped out" in the industry parlance) and the fabrication phase starts.

Chip fabrication involves taking this printer's block, loading it up into all that expensive equipment at the chip fabrication facility. This equipment will start to run the imprints of this printer's block on a pizza-shaped circular wafer material. Each wafer is imprinted with several copies of this printer's block. Each imprint is a fully fabricated chip, called a "die." The wafer is then cut into individual dies, each die is placed in a black-colored hard package with pins sticking out from all it sides.

This black-colored package, either rectangular or square in shape, with metallic pins sticking out from two or all four of its sides is what we are most familiar with as an IC – for integrated circuit – or is also called a "chip."

RECURRING AND NON-RECURRING COSTS

The *design and development* phase for an ASIC chip may take anywhere from 9 to 18 months whereas the manufacturing phase is in the order of 2 to 3 months long for the first silicon samples.

The cost structure of these two phases is such that the design and development costs are typically one-time costs or *non recurring (NRE) costs.* This is because once the final electronic layout file is generated and approved for the dispatch to the fabrication plant, the design and development phase comes to a completion and no more investment is needed on the design.

The costs in the fabrication phase, however, depend on how many runs in the chip production are required to fulfill customer orders.

The fabrication costs are calculated on a per chip basis. This is because each chip has to be fabricated, packaged, and tested *individually* before shipping to the customer. In other words, the manufacturing costs are *recurring costs,* recurring with each customer order, and depend on the sales volumes of the product.

It is normal in semiconductor chip companies to have dedicated operations managers keeping a close watch on the rising and falling costs of the various line items that go into the overall chip cost. As such, the recurring and non recurring costs are combined into a *cost of goods sold* (COGS) quantity and this COGS is used to compute the gross margin.

For example, often it is the responsibility of the chip company to procure the raw materials such as wafers and the masks and supply them to the fabrication plant. Depending on the process technology the costs of these wafers and masks can be exorbitantly higher – sometimes running into millions of dollars if it is a latest process technology under 90nm - for a startup semiconductor company to bear. The operational staff has to negotiate with their counterparts at the fabrication plant to work out a way to mitigate these costs.

Also of prime importance is the die yield – the number of good working dies that can be rolled out from each wafer. As the wafer costs go up, it is important to have a high die yield to maximize on the production efficiency.

The size of the die, which is a function of the complexity of the design and the efficiency of the design implementation, directly affects the number of dies per wafer.

In addition, the choice of the package, the packaging costs, the costs of testing the packaged IC, all of these must be factored in as accurately as possible to have a firm understanding of the chip costs.

A realistic estimation of the complete chip cost requires answering several questions such as these and drawing from a variety of resources up and down the manufacturing supply chain partners.

AN EXAMPLE

Consider the following hypothetical example of a cost estimation of an ASIC chip for a certain signal processing protocol.

The system architects have laid out the entire system block diagram on a piece of paper and have made an initial estimate of the total gate count required. So the die size estimate is done.

Let us say that it takes about 9 months to build the ASIC and get it to the tapeout stage, with 20 designers working full time – that is 180 man months.

Chip Development NRE Cost Estimates

People Costs		Infrastructure Costs	
Project Duration	9 months	EDA license cost	$100k
Development Staff	20 full time	No. of computers	20
Average cost	$12k per man-month	Cost per computer	$2k
Total duration	180 man-months	Computing cost	$40k
Resource cost	$2.2M (180 x $12k)	Misc	$60k
Combined NRE Cost	$2.2M+$200k = $2.4M	Total infrastructure cost	$200k

NRE COST

With a conservative cost estimate of $12k/man-month, the people cost amounts to $2.2M ($12k/man-month times 180 man months.) A reasonable approximation for the combined costs for the EDA tools ($100k total for 10 "seats" of the software tools), the computers the designers use ($2k x 20 computers = $40k) and the laboratory equipment can lead to $200k. Together with the $2.2M, we have $2.4M. This would be the one-time NRE cost of the ASIC chip development.

MANUFACTURING COST

Next, for the manufacturing cost estimate, we start with the total gate count estimate from the system architecture phase. The choice of process technology itself is also driven by the performance requirements of the system. Given the gate count estimate, it is simply a matter of mathematics to arrive at the overall *die size* – in square mm – for this given process.

Next, you look at how many dies of this size can be carved out of a wafer – available in 200mm or a 300mm diameter sizes – and this is a measure of the ratio of the effective wafer area over the die area. The number of dies that this ratio gives is normally weighted with a die yield factor. The closer this die yield is to 100% the better.

Typical numbers are process dependent and range from 50% to 80%.

Regardless, in the final analysis a numeric figure representing the *number of good dies per wafer* can be arrived at through this back of the envelope calculation.

For example, a 200mm diameter wafer will result in about a 1000 dies each of 30 sq. mm in size. A die yield factor of 75% would reduce this number and make good dies per wafer to 750. If the wafer cost is $2k, then an untested, unpackaged die cost would is around $2.67. When you add packaging and testing for each die, then the overall cost per chip will easily go up to $3.50.

For a customer order for 100k chip parts then the *manufacturing costs alone* to fulfill this order is 100k x $3.50 = $350k.

Again, keep in mind that the overall investment on the part of the business unit to fulfill this order is the *combined* cost totaling $2.75M, comprising of the one-time NRE cost of $2.4M, a time period of about 10 months, the chip manufacturing cost of $350k and a few other miscellaneous costs that we haven't factored in our example.

Regardless of how the numbers work out, the point of the above illustration is to show the details involved in building the business case for the new product initiative. In the final analysis, the chip cost estimates are drawn next to the projected volumes over the period of the ensuing ten or twelve quarters.

BREAK-EVEN POINT

In the above example, to manufacture 100k chips, it costs $350k. This is in addition to the one time NRE cost of $2.4M. If the chip price is set at $10, then just to recoup the development costs of $2.4M alone, the company would have to ship at least 240k chip units to recoup the costs of manufacturing these 240k chips at the rate of $350k per 100k units.

In other words, the chip company will have to generate a combined revenue of over $3.2M ($2.4M + $840k) and *sell close to a quarter million chips just to break even on the NRE costs!.* This is assuming that the ASIC chip works the very first time it was taped out and sent to fab, which is almost never the case.

To convince the business unit to approve for the new product, the combined marketing and engineering team managers would have to make a pretty good business case. They must show that there is enough customer traction and demand to justify for significantly higher volumes that are required to make the entire business unit profitable.

IN CONCLUSION

So we conclude the economics context. Product definition done, business case made and now it is time to start thinking about the design wins. For that we turn, in the next two chapters, to the customer context.

15

THE CUSTOMER CONTEXT

When you are in charge of a new product that has just passed through the PRB approval, the technological context has already started its forward movement towards the customer context. What this means is, from the circle of execution viewpoint, the immediate goal you should achieve is to secure a design win.

While a design win is the goal that you want to get to, the way you get there is to engage with a customer. In fact, there are two fundamental reasons why you want to engage with a customer:

First, because a customer provides a design win.

Second, a customer will help the marketing manager get to this design win by giving access to their product requirements early on.

While the design and development, product quality and operations groups are busy with the day-to-day logistics of the silicon tape-out, testing and re-spin, there is a whole host of *business* activities that sales and marketing teams are engaged in. These activities constitute the customer context.

REFERENCE DESIGN

The process of customer engagement starts with identifying who the potential customers are in your market segment. While you are doing that, the most important tool you have, to attract the attention of these potential customers, is a *reference design*.

The extent to which a reference design determines the success or failure of a semiconductor company is not usually understood by most semiconductor startups.

This is perhaps understandable. It is an easy trap for most startups to think that since they are a semiconductor chip company, all they need to do is to build these chips, make them work and they are done!

The problem with this assumption is, no one on your customer side would know how to use this chip without the reference design. Sending them tons of documents with datasheets, layout diagrams and pin-out specification only does so much.

So, as a rule of necessity, a semiconductor chip company almost always plans – and should plan if it doesn't – to build a reference design with their chips on it.

Exactly what is a reference design?

A reference design is a prototype board which performs the intended application for which this chip is built. For example, a semiconductor company making the chips for the WLAN communication protocol would build an example prototype board – with all the necessary behavior that is expected of the WLAN router box – and uses this prototype board to demonstrate to all the parties interested that the semiconductor chip works as advertised.

As a result, a reference design serves a singularly important purpose of demonstrating to a potential customer the functionality of the chip in a show-and-tell manner.

The design of the reference prototype board is usually scheduled well in advance of the availability of the first silicon samples. By the time the first samples of the silicon start to arrive from the packaging and testing facility, a bulk of the design for the reference prototype board is already completed, tested and verified for circuit electronics.

The first task of the product development team, as soon as it has a working silicon in their hand, is to place it in the reference prototype board and test its functionality.

It is only when this reference prototype board is verified that the sales and marketing teams are equipped to take concrete steps to engage with the potential customers. Until a working reference design is available, no startup semiconductor company will be successful in sustaining the interest of their potential customers, no matter how jazzy their presentation slides are or how compelling their marketing pitches are.

OEM AND ODM

For a chip company, although the goal is to eventually *win a socket* in the OEM box, there are several ways this win can be achieved. Each involves a third party in the equation, namely an ODM (original design manufacturer) or a CEM (contract electronic manufacturer).

A simple way to remember how an ODM is different from an OEM is as follows: an OEM is a name-brand company and orients itself primarily to creating innovative next generation product ideas. An ODM, on the other hand, concentrates on the low-cost manufacturing of the product. In a way an ODM is like a contract manufacturer, and sometimes also outsources the manufacturing work to the contract manufacturer.

An OEM's focus is more on marketing to their service provider and retail customers. Substantial investments are made to maintain close relationships with these customers, all with a goal to secure next generation product requirements and coming up with a design for such products.

In a typical case an OEM of this type would have nothing to do with the manufacture of this design. The OEM will outsource this manufacturing and product building task entirely to a contract manufacturer. In this case an OEM and contract manufacturer are in an exclusive relationship with each other.

There are some OEMs however, which put in place a business model wherein they would have nothing to do with either the design or the manufacture of the product – they just focus on creating product features and requirements that make them competitive. These OEMs differentiate themselves by providing a low-cost alternative to a name-brand product. These OEMs will turn to ODMs for their design *and* manufacturing needs because of a crucial advantage an ODM brings to the table: the low cost advantage.

It is easy to understand why these OEMs find an ODM business model consistent with their needs. A bulk of the cost to produce a next-generation product goes into the research, design and development, while manufacturing cost per unit are significantly smaller on a volume basis. So an OEM which wants to differentiate itself as a low-price alternative would do well to relegate most of its design, development and manufacturing to a low-cost manufacturing partners such as an ODM.

The ODM model is dominant in Taiwan. These companies have revolutionized the economics of modern electronics industry by their cheap product manufacturing costs and their ability to rapidly commoditize any product area that they get into.

While the ODM does have a considerable cost advantage in *manufacturing*, it is a fact that they continue to lag behind a traditional OEM in the areas of design and development.

Because of this, there is a strong tendency on the part of an ODM to look elsewhere for the design skills. As a consequence, an ODM would typically exert enormous pressure on their suppliers – the semiconductor chip supplier being one of them - to compensate for this lack of design expertise by requiring the chip supplier to provide a *manufacture-ready* package for the chip.

ENGAGE, DON'T OVERWHELM, THE CUSTOMER

If your company is a startup, your search for a customer starts with hiring the right people in sales and marketing positions. This does not necessarily mean that you hire only those people who have big Rolodexes™.

It means that you look for people who have a good grasp not only of the business of the semiconductors from a macro point of view, but also a particular mindset.

The context of engaging the customer requires that the individual should be able to peel open the layers of market trends, industry opinions, and false patterns that your competitors deliberately create to confuse.

The first step in engaging with a potential customer is to actually secure some face-time with them so that they are willing to listen to your pitch.

Most first-timers to semiconductor marketing, especially those who are transitioning from an engineering position, would not think that just getting in front of a potential customer itself involves a lot of leg work. Because nobody talks about it, it is often assumed that someone, either a CEO or a COO would have a list of all the potential customers. They would just hand down these lists to sales and marketing people and a simple phone call would start the process. Far from it.

It takes considerable investment of time, effort and travel to secure a list of "*leads*" that could potentially be interested in what you have to offer.

Assuming you are successful in this you will start with introducing yourselves. This is typically done by using a set of presentation foils. The key to start a productive interaction in any such meeting is to keep *your* presentation short and precise, conclude quickly and leave the rest of the meeting for the potential-customer to query you.

QUALIFYING THE CUSTOMER

The objective of this initial meeting is for you, as a representative of the semiconductor company to *qualify* this customer.

Qualifying a customer simply means that you have methodically examined the customer at this initial stage against a few set criteria to determine if *you* are willing to engage this customer. Implicit in this position is a possibility of turning this potential-customer away if they don't qualify.

It may appear as strange that you are actually even thinking about turning away a customer. It is understandable. All of us are consumers in our lives. If we want to buy anything we just go to a nearest store and unless there is a specific reason for the store-owner to not to let you in, it is hard for us to imagine the store-owner turning us – *anyone* – down.

But this is where business marketing, and especially semiconductor marketing, differs.

In the business of semiconductors the value chain is so complex and intricate that a relationship between a customer and a vendor that is tied *only* at the end-point of a finished-product handoff is usually *almost always insufficient* for this product to be successful.

Every successful marketing and sales individual in this industry has amassed their successes by virtue of their appreciation of this insight. Every relationship we strike with a customer is a commitment that we expect to last long, benefiting several generations of our product. At the same time, this commitment imposes certain upfront guidelines. We want to make sure that the potential customer in front of us not only needs to be convinced of our product and technology. But in turn, this customer must be qualified to ensure that we can count on him for an honest business and the company's forward movement.

Qualifying a potential customer involves bringing up specific questions and leading them to address these questions during the course of your meeting with them. Here is a list of a few such key questions.

1. Is the business model compatible to engage in a non-competitive manner?
2. What kind of resources they are ready to put on this project?
3. Evaluate their financial and staying power.
4. What kind of relationship they have with the rest of the industry players?
5. Is there a schedule match?
6. What is the opportunity *for you*? Can you articulate it? Can you write a two paragraph statement on what the opportunity is?
7. How big is the opportunity?
8. How near-term or long-term is the opportunity?
9. What kind of support they need?
10. Why are they interested in you? Do you have something that merely helps them or is what you have essential to their business model?

One other reason why you want to engage in a customer qualification exercise is, more often than not, *this is the only way you will know anything worthwhile about your potential-customer.*

What you learn from this session depends on the kind of business model of the potential-customer i.e., whether they are an OEM, an ODM or a contract manufacturer. Of course you will engage other kinds of customers and partners such as the IP vendors, module makers, middleware vendors etc. In all these cases, the same guidelines apply.

Below we will elaborate further on each of these questions.

IS THE BUSINESS MODEL COMPATIBLE TO ENGAGE IN A NON-COMPETITIVE MANNER

For a semiconductor chip company, the natural customer is an OEM company which makes boxes such as a DVD player, a computer or a digital camera. In this case the business models of the semiconductor company and the box maker are compatible.

Often times, however, it may not be clear what the potential customer's business model is. You need to dig deeper into their company website or their product brochures well before the meeting to figure out exactly what they make: boxes or semiconductors? Or both?

For example a company such as Cisco may be well known for making networking boxes. But in a few markets, as in the WLAN, they also make semiconductor chips. As long as you are speaking to a group from Cisco that is in the business of box making and not semiconductor chips, you have a potential customer. Nevertheless you should be watchful here. This type of company, which makes both the semiconductors and system boxes, can pose tricky problems in *how much* you divulge to the box maker group. There is always a danger that someone might slip in a piece or two of crucial information to their semiconductor colleagues which you wouldn't want that to happen.

WHAT KIND OF RESOURCES THEY ARE READY TO PUT ON THIS PROJECT

Regardless of the financial strength, stature and the reputation of the potential-customer company, you should always try to get a feel for how serious they are *on this project*. This measure is usually reflected in the make up of the development staff that is assigned to this project. The larger the staff (resources) this potential-customer is willing to commit, or has already committed to this project, the higher this project is on their priority list. This is a good sign because as the project progresses (assuming this prospect is engaged), the strain on your own support staff is not unduly high.

EVALUATE THEIR FINANCIAL STRENGTH

Never hesitate to ask, if they have not already presented this information in their presentation foils, how financially sound they are. Whether this potential-customer is a startup or a medium-sized company or a large public company, it always comes down to the question of what kind of financial commitment the potential-customer is willing to make.

WHAT KIND OF RELATIONSHIP THEY HAVE WITH THE REST OF THE INDUSTRY PLAYERS

A potential customer can have an ongoing relationship with a competitor of yours which they may not tell you even if you ask them. Although this fact alone should not stop you from engaging with this customer, it is always instructive to feel this out.

IS THERE A SCHEDULE MATCH? HOW NEAR-TERM OR LONG-TERM IS THE OPPORTUNITY?

Ask them what *their* product schedules are. Typically box maker OEMs – especially consumer electronics OEMs – have set schedules that they plan out four to six quarters in advance. They need to place their products on the retail shelves in time for the major consumer spending seasons, such as starting in November for Christmas and late summer or beginning of Fall for back-to-school.

Most often a single data point from the customer, such as the target production quarter, should be enough. You can work backwards and estimate accurately the timeframe during which they expect to have a working silicon sample in their hand to complete their box development before shipping it off to the retail channels.

Keep in mind that these OEM schedules are driven by their own end markets and *not* by their chip supplier readiness. The cut-throat competition in the end markets is such that an OEM doesn't really care who supplies them the chips, as long as they are supplied in a timely, reliable and cost effective manner. If *you* want to be their number one chip supplier, then you must have your silicon working by this timeframe so you can beat the competition on your way to securing a design win with this OEM.

WHAT IS THE OPPORTUNITY FOR YOU? CAN YOU ARTICULATE IT? CAN YOU WRITE A TWO PARAGRAPH STATEMENT ON WHAT THE OPPORTUNITY IS?

Quite often it happens that these initial meetings with potential-customers have a tendency to be all over the map. It is easy to be swamped in these sessions with all kinds of information from the customer about their market space and their history, origins and their success stories.

All of this preamble can easily make you lose focus on the key issue, which is to identify *what* the business is between both the parties. Not only that, you have to identify this business *in specific terms*. This identification starts with you asking yourselves what is the nature of the opportunity *for you*. That you and your potential-customer are in the same room means you both are addressing the same broader market. But just because there is this commonality does not mean that you have identified what and where *your* opportunity is. Identifying your opportunity takes some amount of legwork and delineating *who sells to whom and how the money is made*. Essentially you should know what is the buyer-seller opportunity and craft a relationship around that.

HOW BIG IS THE OPPORTUNITY?

Size the business opportunity in terms of unit volumes and pricing power. For a chip company, this depends on the type of end markets such as high volume and low volume markets. As a general trend, any time the chip product is directly used in an end-consumer product, it tends to be a high volume market. Laptop computers, cell phones, WLAN routers and adapter cards, all are high volume markets. On the other hand, the infrastructure, the equipment that service providers and business use is likely a lower volume but higher price per unit market.

GEARING FOR DESIGN WIN

If the customer prospect passes all the above criteria and is qualified, it is now time to set the sights on the design win.

How, then, does the context for the design win unravel itself? That is the focus of the next chapter.

16

THE DESIGN-IN

In this chapter we will explore the customer context from the viewpoint of a design win. More specific, we are interested in the process of engaging the prospective customer in a beta program. This beta phase is also called as a *design-in* phase. When the design-in phase successfully results in a substantial customer order for the chip parts, we refer to it as a *design win* for the chip.

A marketer's primary job is to be successful in turning the not-yet-economical quality of the product into a purely economic quality. As such we have already seen the marketing function as a specific responsibility to connect these two contexts. The marketer accomplishes it by transplanting the product from a *technological* context of the design environment into a *customer's* context in which this product solves a well-defined problem.

While this is the goal that must be achieved to be successful, the *means* to get there are harder to put in place. One of the most challenging aspects of the marketer's job is in securing the confidence and the agreement of the members of the engineering group. Without an agreement between the marketing and the engineering teams, no chip company can succeed in deploying a winning solution in the market. It is here in the nexus between marketing and engineering that the engine of execution located. It is the responsibility of the marketing function to ensure that this engine runs smoothly. The debilitating effect of every other failure in the company is either amplified or diminished by what happens at this nexus.

EXPLODING DESIGN COMPLEXITY

Sure enough there are other areas in any organization that are equally responsible for the success or failure of the company. Nevertheless, the specific nature of the high-technology semiconductor business is such that it tends to move every issue that is crucial to the survival of the company squarely *into* the nexus between these two groups.

This specific nature has to do with the high degree of complexity of the chip product. The market conditions in the electronics industry have come to change so fast that the time-to-market pressures do not allow enough time for this complexity to settle in.

As a result, the product design teams rarely get an opportunity to wrap their arms around the entire chip system on a day-to-day basis. Without sufficient time to work with the full chip system, laid out from front to back, it is often near-impossible to ensure that all the possible glitch-prone areas are well identified.

To manage it, the engineering teams typically break this design complexity into smaller sub-tasks and bind these sub-tasks into a framework of costs, upfront planning and tight budgetary control. Chip design teams are required to put an extraordinary degree of focus, teamwork to disperse this complexity into such manageable subtasks and bring these pieces back together as a working entity.

By this very act of breaking it down into discrete and fixed tasks with clear boundaries, the technological context becomes diametrically opposed to the continuously changing, dynamic, and an amorphous nature of the economic context. It is up to the marketing function to manage these diametrically opposing forces in such a way that the technological context of the product is rapidly being transformed into the economic context *within* the given time to market window for the company to be successful.

The beta phase is where these opposing forces are prominently seen at play.

THE BETA PHASE CONTEXT

When a prospective OEM or ODM customer and the chip company decide to work together, the events up to this stage would have progressed more or less goes along the following lines.

The prospective customer has independently, following their own business objectives, made plans to build a box-level product. And they are in the market looking for a chip supplier. As this is a new application area, there are quite a few startups, including yours, *and* large companies racing to put out the best chip product into the market *first*.

Through a series of meetings and diligent follow-ups, your marketing and technical teams were successful in raising this prospective customer's interest in your chip. Your marketing team, after a series of customer qualification stages (we discussed the topic of qualifying the customer earlier in this book) is convinced that the volume of units of these boxes that this customer-prospect claimed he could sell are more or less founded and valid. Now it is time to get a joint agreement in place and start to work together.

The actual mechanics of how this joint project gets underway are quite straightforward. The prospective OEM customer forms a small internal group of engineers, system architects and a project coordinator. As a chip vendor, you would set up a similar project coordinator counterpart on your end.

To kick-start the project, typically the prospective customer will request for the following: a set of development boards, the software that is used to program your chip, a set of documents from your engineering group with the electrical and functional characteristics of the chip.

Armed with these tools, the beta-customer would then start out on a critical task of building the overall system on this "reference" board. This overall system would comprise of various components on the reference board that are required for whatever the application that the box product is intended for. The chip from your company will play a central role and an important part of the box's components list, also referred to as the bill-of-materials.

SUPPORT IS EVERYTHING

If the semiconductor chip company is a startup with the first product heading towards a tapeout, then *keep in mind that you don't yet have the chip in your hand* at the time of this beta customer engagement. All anybody has is a set of specifications that your engineering team has developed, a "data-sheet" of the product with the parameter values generated from the computer simulations, the interface diagram, the pin-out diagram, and the footprint of the chip.

So the approach that any beta-customer would take at this stage is to focus their team's efforts on building the *rest of the system that is around* your chip. Until a working version of your chip is available in customer's laboratory, the socket for your chip on the reference board remains a simple placeholder.

To be able to build this overall system without your chip on the board, the customer engineers building this board will make certain assumptions based on the information contained in the datasheets you supply them.

Throughout this customer engagement there will be a steady inflow of requests from the customer on various aspects of your chip, primarily to learn more about this chip. The project coordinators on both sides would monitor the project carefully.

Regular once or twice a week conference calls between the engineers on both sides are common. This entire beta phase is an extremely critical time for both the parties. The beta-customer is taking a high risk, in betting their product development on an assumption that your chip, when it comes back from the fab, works as advertised. If the chip comes back with a bug, then the whole project is delayed by a few months, until that bug is fixed.

When this happens, the OEM customer often misses the market window as a result of which they either cancel the product or select your competitor's chip. Either way, you as a chip company, is the loser.

Notice how quickly the context for the semiconductor chip product is changing.

From the technological context of the specification, the standards, the validation suite, the test plan, the development environment, the project plan, the budgetary controls and so on, there is a steady shift in the utility of your product as it is rapidly being transplanted into the overall system context.

It does not stop here.

This product must emerge out of *this* overall system context once again to step into a still another context, the economic context, which starts to take on *its* existence when this customer start to generate revenue from this box.

In this interplay of emergences, it is important to note that this overall system context, which appears as a customer context to you, is still the technological context *for the customer.* In customer's eyes, as long as his product is in the system-building phase, as long as he is still in the process of making the chip vendor selection decision, and as long as the various field trials are still being underway, his box product has not yet attained neither *his* customer's context nor his economic context. In turn, as a chip maker, your economic context does not materialize unless and until the customer's economic context materializes.

BEWARE OF THAT FAULT-LINE, AGAIN

At the outset, given the uncertainty of the chip's status throughout the design-in phase, the beta-customer has nowhere else to turn to except the chip company to remove these uncertainties. The OEM company is continuously evaluating the chip company's progress to ensure that the chip product fits well into the overall system context with as few setbacks as possible.

Although a bulk of the chip technical specifications are already baked into the building blocks of the semiconductor, way back when the technological context was originating, there is a continuous incoming stream of specific requests for a change in the specification. These requests constitute the bulk of the requirement or feature changes for the product.

Along with these requirement changes are the constant back and forth of the support-related queries to address the crisis moments, those unforeseen turns in the project. All this requires a careful handholding of the beta customer by the chip company marketing and applications support personnel. After all, it is the *customer's* overall system context that is the source of the future life for the chip product. Not only that, this system context is also the launching pad into the economic context for both the parties. If there is a time when the goals and purposes of two companies, a chip company and a beta OEM customer, are to be aligned near perfectly, the beta phase is usually it.

The terminology used to describe these two types of incoming requests are different. In general, any change request that requires a change in the chip product itself and directly impacts the chip product in this way is referred to as an *engineering change order* or an ECO for short.

The other type of request which does not require a direct change in the chip product but however impacts the engineering team's time and effort is termed as *a support request*.

Whatever may be the nature of this request, it first enters the company through a communication from the beta-customer to the customer-facing members of the chip company, the application support engineers and marketing personnel.

At the same time, it also enters the unseen dichotomy of marketer's opportunity cost vs. the engineer's budgetary cost and slowly starts to act in the background, sight unseen.

THE LANGUAGE PROBLEM

However, as straightforward as this model may appear, it belies another underlying dichotomy separating the marketing from engineering, a dichotomy that creates a *barrier* in the proper handling of this request. This barrier lies in the *difference* in the *language and terms of the assessment* used by marketing and engineering.

To understand this barrier let us trace the path of this request as it is handled.

Whether this is a request for a modification or an addition of a certain feature into the chip, or a support request that requires the engineering team to lend a hand to the application support group, an often observed reaction from the engineering manager goes along the following:

"Now that the product development is underway, it is important to keep the schedule and costs according to the initial budget. Who pays the price if the product is delayed because we took a diversion to entertain this new request? We will accommodate it in the next revision of the chip. These guys are not the only customers out there, right? We will have plenty of customers who will buy this chip when we build it. It just takes too much of re-architecting the chip for us to even think about doing it, so forget it!"

On the other hand, a typical marketing manager's reaction to these initial responses from the engineering manager go like this:

"But the competition already has it and we *know* that our customer is running a parallel beta project with their chips. If we don't commit to this feature the game is practically over. This is our number one customer prospect with large volumes and we can't afford to upset these guys. What do you mean you'll slip the schedule? We want both this feature AND deliver it on time. Our customer doesn't care, and shouldn't have to care, how difficult or how long it takes to implement this feature, they just want it so we'll have to give it to them!"

MANAGE THE DIFFERENCE, DON'T BRUSH IT ASIDE

Notice how different is the language and the criteria for the success is for these two groups: the planned schedule, budgetary cost, reluctance to digress from a fixed plan of the engineering manager versus the competition, the customer, the prospect for large volumes etc., of the marketing manager.

The ultimate result of these differences is, *neither of the groups trust the estimates of the other* because the criteria used to arrive at these estimates are so strange to one another's worldview, that there is no common ground on which they both can stand and translate these criteria from one world to another.

To be sure, nothing of what we just laid out is new to the people in the chip industry.

In fact good chip companies actually identify this barrier and put in place the expertise to handle exactly these kinds of situations. You'll see roles such as system architects, product architects, solution architects straddling the marketing and engineering groups, filling in that nebulous zone where the bulk of the interaction between marketing and engineering lies.

However, the efficacy of these roles depend largely on the structure of the organization. If a system architect is simply a glorified design engineer with no contextual experience with markets, it often results in just the channeling of the conflict and not the resolution of the conflict.

As such this difference in the language originates from the original difference in the worldviews that we have already identified. But this language difference now strikes deeper, creating fault lines in the terms of the assessment, the rationale for making a decision one way or the other and the language that is used to articulate. So much so that often the resolution of what should be done with the request takes up enormous amounts of time for these decision differences to sort themselves out.

Herein lies a root of the problem. If you look closer it becomes clear that this time consuming behavior has *very little to do* with the complexity of the request itself.

Almost all of the back and forth on the decision itself is an internal struggle, just to manage this difference in the worldviews and the ensuing language differences.

Moreover, if you are not aware of this phenomena it appears to the organization that there is really nothing wrong with the process and that all such time consuming behavior is *natural to the vagaries of the chip development!*

In this manner, there develops a false assumption which quickly takes its roots in the culture. It strikes deep into the makeup of the company during its formative stages. It digs deeper in the technological context of the product and if not managed well, actually *prevents* the product from being transplanted smoothly into the overall system context of the customer and subsequently to the economic context for both the chip company and their OEM customer.

PART 4

THE CRAFT AND THE MINDSET

17

THE
REQUIREMENTS
CRAFT

One of the first questions to ask when thinking about a high technology product such as a semiconductor chip is, what do you *know* about it? Equally importantly, do you have this knowledge in a form that lets you *communicate* it to others.

Getting to know what you need to build the product starts first with an appreciation of the difference between a *specification* and a *requirement*.

Specifications are what make the product actually work. Requirements are what fulfill the product to interact in the customer's context.

This is a crucial difference.

In other words, the requirements are what the customer *wants* to see as features in the product. Specifications are the details of *how* a requirement can be implemented. One of the unspoken skills a good marketer must develop is to instinctively distinguish between the *what* and the *how*, to cast his eye squarely on the *what* and the tradeoffs around this requirement.

SELF-REQUIRING VS. VALUE-BUILDING

Too often a product is ill-defined because of a basic misunderstanding of what a requirement is. Most high technology designers and marketers mistakenly think that a requirement is just a customer expectation. They forget that if the customer is already expecting a feature, then what is new?

In this sense, it is helpful to categorize a product attribute into two groups: a *self-requiring* attribute and a *value-building* attribute. Let us elaborate what we mean.

Think of an every day electronics product, such as a mobile phone. We carry it with us because we *know* that with this mobile phone in our possession we have the capability of a phone conversation wherever we go. The moment we think of this phone, we *already* expect this capability. The monthly subscription fee we pay for that mobile service, for that particular phone of our choice, is to purchase precisely this capability.

In other words, the basic functionality of a mobile phone *is already priced* into our expectations. This is the minimum requirement. Without this expectation in our minds, we would not approach an electronics store to buy a phone. In fact, without this expectation, there is no demand, no market and in fact no one would manufacture these phones at all!

In other words, the capability of the phone to connect to another user over the air is a *self-requiring* feature. This self-requiring feature is an absolute necessity for the phone to exist in the marketplace.

Now take another feature of the same phone, such as an address book or a built-in camera. These are *value-building* features. Neither of these is absolutely necessary for the phone to work *as a phone*, but these features are what enable the phone to differentiate itself in the customer context.

All the technology, both hardware and software, that is needed for a product to function *as that product*, belongs to the self-requiring category. Any differentiating, news-worthy feature belongs to the value-building category. Anything that is priced in is a self-requiring feature. That which is a pleasant surprise is a value-building feature.

A self-requiring feature merely enables the product to exist in the marketplace. A value-building feature enables the *forward movement* from the technological context to the customer context and eventually to the economic context.

Of course, as time passes, all the users come to expect this value-building feature to be there already, so a value-building feature is reduced to a self-requiring feature. A new value-building feature must be defined for differentiation. This is how commoditization manifests.

Language, Again

An important distinction between a self-requiring feature and a value-building feature lies in the suitability of a particular language to express the feature.

By nature, a value-building feature thrives in a customer context, and hence it requires a non-technical language to express that feature. A self-requiring feature, on the other hand, mostly resides in the technological context and the language used to express this feature is highly technical.

For example, the type of the embedded microprocessor, the size and the type of the memory used, the type of the peripheral bus interfaces the processor requires, all these are self-requiring features, which make sense only to the designers and the architects of the technological context.

By and large, a tendency endemic to the high technology industry is its inability to recognize this distinction. End consumers are routinely presented with new products in a jargon that is ill-suited to express a value-building feature. VGA monitor? 512MB DDR

SDRAM? 192KHz/24-bit audio DAC? DVD+/-RW/DVD Drive, DVD-ROM Drive? What possible meaning do these descriptions convey to the end user?

Every one of these is really a description of *how* the manufacturer intends to deliver a particular value. *A 512MB DDR SDRAM is by itself not a description of a value-building feature.* The real value-building feature here is the faster speed of the computer.

High technology sector continues to ignore the unaddressed problem of this language translation. The challenge for the marketer continues to be that of this language *translation* from a specification, from a self-requiring feature jargon to a value-building feature description.

WHERE DO PRODUCT REQUIREMENTS COME FROM

So where do product requirements come from? Let us see how they are put together in a real semiconductor company.

STANDARDS

Gathering product requirements – and it really is *gathering* from a variety of different contexts – requires a certain amount of skill, a willingness to get in front of the customers and listen to them. However, if you are building a standards-based chip, then these standards documents themselves act as the immediate source for a *basic* set of requirements.

As your customers also have access to these standards documents, they design the features for their boxes around the stipulations of these standards documents.

As a consequence your customers *already expect* your chip to support most of what is in the standard.

This expectation is already built into the customer thinking *even before you and the customer have communicated on this matter.*

In a nutshell, expect the customer to assume that your chip will be fully compliant to the standards. That is the first requirement your product must fulfill.

Keep in mind that these expectations in the customer's mind were formed without your involvement. An OEM customer would have similar expectations from any chip vendor, i.e., you and your competitor, to be considered as a major supplier, making these standards-based requirements as a *must-haves* for all the chip vendors.

In other words, you should expect no differentiation play by just implementing these standards.

FROM CUSTOMER

Next in line are the requirements that are gathered using explicit communication with the customer.

These explicitly communicated requirements are perhaps the most important element in making the product market-worthy and competitive.

A straightforward way to build these requirements is to simply pick up the phone and talk to the customer. As in the chip company, the OEM company also has a product marketing manager who is the an appropriate individual for this conversation. The OEM product marketing manager is responsible to fulfill the requirements for their box product and your chip would be an enabler to fulfill features at the box level.

A chip company, even a startup with paltry financial resources, invests money to send its personnel to the trade shows and conferences. This is to give an opportunity for the marketing people to establish contact with their counterparts at their customer companies, and exchange names, contact addresses, phone numbers etc.

Like anything else in high technology businesses, the OEM company's preferences, on which supplier to use, are driven by their choice-making and the decision-making marketers. Tracking their preferences involves a huge amount of search costs which these trade shows can help minimize.

PRODUCT RFQs

If your product is already in use by the OEM, then depending on the relationship you have with this OEM customer, it is possible that these OEM customers include you in their circulation of what are known as RFQs – request-for-quotation – documents.

The RFQs are a set of requirements for the products that are in an OEM's development pipeline. By giving you access to such RFQs, these OEM customers prepare you for your next product plan and requirements.

QUARTERLY PRODUCT UPDATES

Another way in which these OEMs might keep you updated is to invite you to exclusive quarterly update meetings in which they would share their product roadmap.

FACE TO FACE

Quite often a more effective way to learn about the requirements for your product is a face to face meeting. To this end, it behooves a product marketing manager to find an opportunity to sit in a room face to face with the customer and methodically engage in a discussion about their product needs.

Throughout this phase of gathering the requirements for the product, it is important to remember that these requirements are for a product that becomes a reality *at some point in the near future*. The product marketing manager's goal is to make this product competitive *at this future time*, i.e., at the time of the product launch.

This means that a feature might appear attractive today, nevertheless a full validation of the competitive nature of the feature is incomplete unless you confirm that its attractiveness remains so at the time *when the customer receives it*. This is one more reason to learn about the OEM customer's schedules *in that same discussion, at that same hour*, while you are talking about the product requirements.

FROM COMPETITION

Quite often the competition ups the ante and puts a feature in a product to gain an advantage over you. This competition feature then becomes a requirement for your product.

DIFFERENTIATORS

In an emerging market sector, new products routinely get assimilated into larger bigger products, often times becoming just a feature in the overall bigger product. For example, the PDA functionality has been commoditized from standalone pure PDA devices to just a check box feature for smart phones. A new product, then, must always satisfy a differentiating requirement, with a value-building feature which creates that much needed forward movement.

MENHIRS OF MIND

Now is a good time to talk about the menhirs of the mind. What are these? These are a peculiar kind of impediments that come in a way of the execution of the requirements-gathering task.

Simply put, a menhir of mind is a bad habit. Like that formless monolith, a menhir lies in the subterranean corners of our mind, creeps up stealthily at crucial moments of execution and leads us astray. Menhirs of the mind are the bad habits that get lodged in our minds and prevent us from thinking clearly. Let's look at a few such menhirs.

First is a seizure of the mind that prevents the marketer (or the engineer) from asking simple straightforward questions of the customer.

Whether one is a marketer or an engineer, there is a widespread malaise that makes one believe that the more specific your questions are, the more you expose your "weakness" of not-knowing-the-answer to this question. Perhaps this comes from an untimely application of the positioning techniques one may learn from marketing text books. Or perhaps this is a reflection of one's own excessive self-consciousness and insecurity.

There are at least two other major impediments that occur commonly in these customer meetings. Both are psychological in nature. First, the marketer talks incessantly. Second, if the marketer has recently migrated from an engineering position, there is a tendency to get fixated on proving one's technical prowess to the customer.

Whatever the reason may be, these menhirs prevent a marketer or an engineer *to ask the customer a question and listen*, thereby permanently losing the opportunity to elicit that precious information on the product requirement from the customer.

THE NATURE OF THESE REQUIREMENTS

We have been repeating over and over again that a fundamental shift in the context of the product from that of a technological to an economic is the key to making the product successful. But when do we know that this shift is indeed taking place?

Not surprisingly, this shift starts to show itself the moment the company commences a conversation with the external world, by way of the sales and marketing people.

An interesting aspect of these conversations with the prospective customers is, there is an almost immediate influx of questions, some merely at the curiosity level and others with a more serious interest, about the product.

As the conversations extend further, soon a subset of these interested OEMs would divulge their product preferences and what they would like to see in the chip product. It is almost as if there is actually a hidden natural tendency for the product to break out of the technological context by attracting the nascent customer context, as customers start to get wrapped up in the idea of the chip product.

When this starts to happen, when this influx of requests for the product literature, of the questions on the product release schedule, and so on, take on a serious note, *the overall system* takes the center stage.

In all practicality, this overall system becomes a stand-in for the customer context.

All that you will now discuss with these seriously interested OEM customers from this point onwards revolves around this overall system. These are the beginnings of the signs of life of the nascent referrals in your product that start to point back to the customer in *their* context.

Having already understood clearly where they can potentially use your chip product, for what problem your product is a solution, these prospective OEM customers would start to use the value-building language. Language such as the *ease-of-use* in designing their application, or what sort of *interfaces* are provisioned for in your chip, *how long* it takes for their application to be ported to your chip platform and so forth.

Slowly but surely, these criteria would start to take hold and strongly influence their impression of your product in their minds as your business relationship starts to solidify.

In a way, there is actually only one requirement that a customer cares about: that this overall system works as advertised when he uses your chip.

18

MANAGE
EXPECTATIONS

Consider the following situation.

You are a product marketing manager in a semiconductor startup that is gearing to release its first chip product. The product has been in the making for a good part of the two years, having gone through several re-spins. During the past four months the engineering team has grown increasingly optimistic that this time around the chip will work. You keep your fingers crossed. You made commitments to your customers that you will deliver the product in the next quarter. Still, a disconcerting feeling in you says that there is an *even chance* of breaking this promise again, if the chip comes back from the fab with bugs.

How would you manage this uncertainty?

Understanding the full ramifications of a situation such as this and following up with unhesitant action forms a fundamental core of the marketing function, of the *execution* function.

THE CONTEXT OF EXPECTATION

First let's look at the context that has already built itself prior to the development of this uncertainty.

Although you knew that the chip could fail, this risk being inherent in any silicon product development, you never let that remote possibility hinder you from actually developing your customer base. In any case it never works like that in the semiconductor industry. If you wait till you are 100% sure of the product availability before you start talking to the customers, you are almost guaranteed to be late to the market and the customers would probably have designed in your competitors.

So you went on to develop your early customer base. Several of your sales and marketing colleagues have worked hard to initiate and cement business relations with OEM and ODM partners. You have something in the works, the super-duper chip for the next generation standard, that these OEM box makers want desperately. They are getting ready to go to market with their product as soon as your chip part is ready.

So there is a natural tendency for the *expectation* to be high in the minds of your OEM customers. As a semiconductor product marketer, this expectations management is an integral part of your job.

As much as *you* believe that you will have a working product in your hand by a certain date, there are a few aspects out of your control that can break this assumption.

First of all, it is not you who is developing the product, your engineering team does that. As you are not in the engineering environment, not in the test laboratory, not in the midst of their middle-of-the-night discoveries of circuit problems and issues, you have to rely on *what they tell you* verbally when you ask them for the status of the product. And they don't necessarily tell you the full story all the time. The accurate status information is especially hard to come by when things are going bad for the engineering team. During moments of a crisis, such as when a chip doesn't work, there is an unavoidable period of denial that any human being goes through during which the surrounding context will suffer from a denial of access to the reality.

So the context has a built-in delay and latency which will translates itself into *an uncertainty for you and your sales colleagues.*

Management of customer expectation consists in taking these internal uncertainties into account and carefully modulating – lowering – the customer expectations, *without* hurting the prospect for the design win.

CALIBRATED OPTIMISM

First, this expectations management starts right from the beginning, way back when you started the product development phase.

The optimism, the energy and the passion with which you go out there in the field and get your prospects lined up, will have to be carefully calibrated, *from the beginning*. The same optimism can come across as a naïve enthusiasm to the customer if you are oblivious to your own limitations in delivering the product. Be realistic in your promises to your customers. Remember, they are also in the same business.

MODULATE EXPECTATIONS

In addition, quite often an impending slip in product schedule calls for a much more methodical and strategic planning to get in front of the crisis. One approach to this starts with an executive-management level review of all the possible scenarios of the chip failure.

Typically it happens as follows:

During the product development cycle, as it nears the tape-out milestone, a risk assessment is made. The VP/Director of Engineering, the chip architects, system architects, the project managers and the product managers evaluate areas in the chip that can go wrong and the extent of the damage in case they do go wrong.

The executive management, along with the marketing and sales force then decide on changing the game plan should these chip failures materialize and formulate what the new game plan is.

As a product marketing manager, it is imperative that you understand these potential chip failures *in terms of what they mean* to the overall functionality of the chip and *in the context* of the overall customer system.

Quite often it is not as straightforward as it seems. This is because the chip failures are usually expressed by the engineering team in the language of the chip specification, in a technical jargon that is insufficient to convey any immediate meaning to the customer.

What you need to do is to *translate* this jargon-filled language into the corresponding customer context language. What particular customer requirement or a value-building requirement is in jeopardy? You should ask questions along the lines of, "Does it mean we won't have this feature A or feature B in case of the chip failure #5?"

The next step involves a careful assessment of each customer's willingness to live with this "de-featured" product.

Note that as a chip vendor you are measured by your customers *first* in terms of how timely you can deliver the product to them and *second* how attractive your product is, over and above the expected functionality of your competitor's product.

Hence, it just *may be* possible to convince at least some of your customers that the performance hit that they take due to the non-availability of a feature is compensated by the on-time delivery of the product.

We say "may be" because your competition is likely to deliver a full-featured product to your customer in which case you are going to have to do much more than simply deliver the sub-optimal product on schedule to achieve the design win. The willingness of the customer to accept a less-than-expected feature-set really depends on *their* product timelines, the availability of a similar chip from your competitor.

Throughout this internal assessment it is important that you are continuously communicating with the customer. You are monitoring the ongoing design-in programs with each one of the customers while at the same time *carefully* modulating their expectations wherever it is needed.

At the conclusion of this exercise, a new game-plan that emerges will most likely be a new business model that calls for a different engagement strategy for a different type of the customer prospect. A customer whose own design expertise is limited might have to be served with a steady and dedicated technical support for the longer term. Hence you may not want to engage them early on. The early customers will be those who have significant design expertise. These will not drain your immediate support resources, otherwise be dedicated to help the engineering team.

When we talk of the execution of a plan and use words such as the "tactical" execution of a strategy, we are referring precisely to these details of how carefully a product marketer articulates in the various verbal, electronic and in presentations, communication with the customer.

Execution of a plan necessarily involves the ability to change people's minds so that they see the benefit of your product in a compelling and clear manner. At the end of the day, winning a customer is demonstrated in these small victories of being able to convince them of a larger benefit in staying with you in spite of the intermittent pitfalls and setbacks. It happens over phone conversations, over email exchanges, by delivering what you promised and over and above, it happens in a slow but steady *building* of trust and value during your rapport with them.

REAL CUSTOMER INFORMATION, NOT *OPINIONS*

Equally important to know are the ways in which this building of trust does *not* happen. Prominent among these is a general tendency to be swayed by your own *opinions* on customer's preferences, mistaking these opinions for real information on customer priorities and letting these untested opinions drive your assessment and strategy.

19

THE EXECUTION MINDSET

There is a well-known anecdote of an exchange between three baseball umpires: "I call them as I see them," said the first. "I call them as they are," claimed the second. The third disagreed, "They ain't nothing till I call them."

Arguments on the market-worthiness of the product are often similar. While the engineering groups are emphatic in their sentiment that they see everything in the product to be market-worthy ("I call them as I see them"), the marketing group generally stands at an arms-length view, turning over the product in a skeptical scrutiny ("I call them as they are.") In the end however, it is the customer who eventually decides whether there is anything there or not ("They ain't nothing till I call them.")

This should not surprise us. In the confluence of the three contexts, i.e., the technological, the overall customer system and the economic, there is a special place for the customer context. It is the forward movement into the customer context that ultimately determines the value of the product. The real question is, "How does one *create* this forward movement?"

Regardless of what creates it, we know one thing for sure: that the *act of decision making* lies at the heart of this forward movement. No forward movement ever takes place without an individual consciously making a decision.

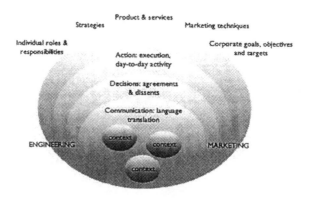

The Microcosm Revisited, a Breeding Ground For Decision-making and Forward Movement

FORWARD MOVING MINDSET

But we knew decisions are not made in vacuum. In fact we suspected, rightly so, that a decision is simply a culmination of agreements and disagreements between individuals. That is why we dug deeper and started this book by deliberately peeling off the outer layer of the technology.

As we cleared off the top layer, the phenomenon of how we all interact with each other within specific contexts began to emerge. Our conviction is, by observing these core phenomena we can better understand the fundamental contexts that drive the decision making, that shape the language and communication and we will eventually comprehend the influences behind the agreements and disagreements.

More than anything, the difference between the forward movement and the status quo is the *mindset of the individual*. Exactly what is that mindset? Is it a collection of techniques? A different way of looking at things? Or is it culture-specific?

Let us look at this mindset.

A Shift In The Perspective

Fault-lines that strike at the heart of the execution engine originate at the bottom of the underlying reality, traverse upwards through human contexts and strike at the heart of the interpersonal communication. Thus we have an ill-comprehended context, a breeding ground for the misapprehensions between individuals. Soon follow inarticulate value propositions, incoherent priorities, and actions that do not translate into the forward movement. This is how execution failures manifest.

What then, are the key ingredients that bring up the forward movement and deliver the company from an execution failure?

To get closer to answering the above question it requires that we take a step *back*. We must step back from our ordinary understanding of the execution as a *collection* of the day-to-day tasks as set by an individual's role and place in the hierarchy of the organization.

So far in our discussion on the engineered products, we have been looking at the objects that we use in our day-to-day lives. We got here by moving *away* from the traditional perspective of the objects around us, and by introducing the quality of referral to each engineered product.

With this slight shift, a whole gamut of latent views of these engineered products came to front. We now experience each engineered product not only as a tool that serves a purpose but also as a harbinger of our very awareness. Having made this shift, we *know* now that every engineered product attains its differentiating quality only when an individual user interacts with it in special way, in a way that is unique to a context.

Now it is time to perform a similar perspective shift in the way we view and understand a traditional high technology task, in fact any task for that matter.

This is where we start to delve into the mindset.

A High Technology Task: a traditional view

In the traditional view, a high technology task, i.e., any task assigned to an engineer or a marketer in a high technology company, is by and large viewed as an activity with certain inputs and outputs.

Take forecasting for example.

Business unit managers are often required to provide, in quarterly updates, the projections of the sales volumes on a product by product basis to the senior management. The tricky aspect of the forecasting is, it often is subject to the vagaries of the business status of the customers.

If you are a startup with the first product still in the making, then these sales forecasts are tightly coupled to the product *availability*. A considerable amount information from the supply chain partners goes into it and what is true today may not be true a month later.

Unless you are a seasoned operations and marketing professional in this area, the task of accurate forecasting can be quite tedious and daunting. You keep staring at a spreadsheet filled with figures that have a tendency to incessantly turn into bland meaningless numbers. The task soon turns into a rigmarole of data gathering and then organizing the data into its document template, in this case a spreadsheet template, elements.

Worse, as this seemingly unending exercise drags on, you are drawn to obsessively try to wield these numbers into a set pattern that lodged itself in your mind. Soon you are lost in the organization of the spreadsheet itself, detached from the larger context in which you began this exercise in the first place. All this happens because somewhere along the way *you lost your way* of the original intent of the task of forecasting and got mired in the limited viewpoint of the spreadsheet itself.

A Different View: Task as an Instrument

The shift in the perspective we propose is intended to keep us aware of this Jekyll-to-Hyde degradation latent in all high technology tasks and steer us as far clear of it as possible.

In this new perspective, we propose to *recast* a high technology task *from* as an activity to as an instrument.

That is, a high technology task is itself an instrument is similar in every way to how we understand the conventional meaning of the term "instrument."

But what are we saying? An instrument is a physical object. How can we equate this physical object with a non-physical entity of a task? Aren't these entirely two different realities? Let us elaborate further.

To be sure, we are not saying anything new. We often see the incarnations of this type of recasting already in all aspects of what we do in high technology companies. For example, whenever we say "let's use this meeting to close the deal," or "let's nail down the specifics in this session," or "let's agree on what the next steps should be," we are implicitly working with a model of the task as an instrument without being aware of it, or to be precise, without *explicitly* being aware of it.

When we say each task is itself an instrument, a question immediately arises: "Is this instrument tangible, like a hammer or a pen?" No. But it has the same qualities. Let's look at an example.

Imagine you are thinking of an upcoming meeting with a customer, and you are representing your company in this meeting.

In the traditional view, this meeting with the customer is a *high technology task* that you do as a part of your job. There is nothing more to be said about it. Of course you are aware that it is important to properly prepare for it, with appropriate message and presentation foils. And your mind is filled with thoughts about this meeting just before you approach this meeting. These thoughts have nothing to do with the *mechanics* of the task. You think of this meeting as the task-at-hand, and you can feel in your mind an anticipation, an expectation, centered on this meeting. Yet, you know somehow that to really feel that you are prepared, there is something else that you need to feel: *that sense of comfort about the meeting as a whole.*

Throughout your preoccupation with this task, from the anticipation when going into the meeting, with the expectations during the course of it and finally to the impressions with which you walk away at the conclusion of this meeting, throughout all this you have just been put through a *two-fold* experience.

First, going into the meeting, you had your eye on the purpose of the meeting. It could be that you want to learn the details on the needs of this customer, or to discuss the terms of a partnership deal that your companies are about to strike.

Second, the *experience* of being in the *actual* meeting itself. Throughout the course of the meeting you and your customer had interchanged information and indicated your mutual preferences on the details of the arrangement. You both articulated your positions in regard to the issue at hand, gathering as much feedback from the other to figure out where you stand and how you can help each other.

Throughout this execution of the high technology task, this two-fold experience has striking similarities to the experience of using an instrument, of using a tool, such as a hammer or a pen. Let us see how.

First, when you reach out and grab a hammer or a chisel, you already know the purpose for which you will use this tool, just like you knew the purpose going into the meeting.

Second, the *actual* experience of using the instrument itself. Whether it is for a simple task of driving in a nail to hang a picture in your living room, or for an elaborate and detail-oriented construction project, you are slowly and steadily progressing towards the end goal, the known purpose, while in unison with the instrument. In the same sense, within the context of the meeting you slowly and steadily worked your way through the course of the meeting, to the conclusion. There is a forward movement and a slow construction of an end result, inherent in these two experiences.

It is in this sense that we draw parallels between a high technology task on one hand and an instrument on the other hand.

RE-INTRODUCING FORWARD MOVEMENT INTO EXECUTION

What do we gain by recasting a high technology task as an instrument?

As it is, we have not changed anything in the way these tasks are executed. We are not interested in any new process or any new technique. What we did is a shift in the perspective, a change in the approach, in how we all *go about* performing these tasks. All we are interested in, *is to re-introduce the forward movement component inherent in any action back into the execution space.*

This is the crux of our effort: we are aiming to re-shape the mindset of the individual by raising the awareness of the forward movement so that the execution of a task is comprehended in a new light.

Why is this forward movement lacking in the traditional view of the high technology execution task? Because a task is always viewed as a *technique*, to be put into practice by *staff resources*, to achieve a set of desirable results.

This is where the problem lies. Just like how the features of a product are meaningless without the individual's context, a task in an execution space cannot simply be viewed as a set of desirable results without according appropriate role to the individual. At the heart of every dysfunctional corporation we find exactly this: no appropriate role being accorded to the individuals.

Whenever individuals in the company are viewed simply as a collective *resource* to put a task into action, the forward movement component disappears. That is when execution problems begin.

Exactly how recasting a task as an instrument brings back the forward movement into the execution? There are several facets to this phenomenon. Let's look at a few of them in some detail.

THE DISTANCE & DECISION MAKING

When we think about it, an instrument is an entity detached and separate from us. We can stare at it at an arms-length distance, yet the moment we start using this instrument, it becomes a part of us *at that moment*.

Implicit in this recasting of the task *as* an instrument is the same idea.

An individual who approaches a task as an instrument implicitly keeps this arms-length distance between him or her and the task at hand. This distance keeps the task from turning into a burden that weighs *on* the individual. High technology executives agree that employees who are able to detach themselves with the emotional turmoil of the day-to-day issues of the project make better decisions.

An individual's decision making ability is inherently tied to the ability to look at the issue at hand from a particular vantage point of view. Informed decision making requires just that, information from all sides of the issue. Successful execution is nothing if not astute decision making. The instrument model of the task provides just that kind of the vantage point of view, by way of this healthy distance.

OWNERSHIP

Casting a task as an instrument gives us an intuitive ownership feeling towards it. We feel much more comfortable knowing that we have an ownership of an instrument, of a tool, whose role it is to aid us, to help us do our job. Rolling up our sleeves and getting right down to it becomes that much more easier with this kind of ownership feeling.

EASE

We feel more at ease *using* a task as an instrument, rather than bearing it as a burden when it is an activity in which we are forced to immerse ourselves. Often times we hear from entrepreneurial minded professionals that they feel choked in big companies. One reason for such an experience is, in big companies it is often difficult to create this distancing space between themselves and the issue at hand. Tasks are given to you with an expectation that you *will perform*, and the instrumentation required is often absent.

TEAMWORK

It is easy to ask someone to show how to use an instrument, if we are stuck at some point. Similarly, we are eager to share our experience of how we learned to use an instrument. On the other hand, when a task is viewed as an activity, any team member who is asked to share often construes it as an additional work which naturally discourages the teamwork.

COMMUNICATION

A high technology task when recast as an instrument encourages communication. You can communicate about the issues, pitfalls and problems you are facing without fear because when you view a task as an instrument, any execution problems reflect more on the instrument and less about you as an individual. We are all naturally less hesitant to ask someone how to use an instrument, any instrument. Hence you don't feel threatened to seek help. You become less defensive. You understand and appreciate that it is not "about you," rather it is about the goal that is to be achieved and all these high technology tasks are simply instruments and tools to get there. You get it.

IMPROVISATION AND CREATIVITY

When you view a high technology task as an instrument, you feel much more free to be creative and to improvise freely on the various ways you can put this instrument to use.

BIG PICTURE

This instrument model also provides that elusive big picture to every employee of the company.

The more an individual is attuned to looking at the high technology tasks as instruments, the more one becomes aware of the purpose and the utility of these instruments. You start asking questions such as "What is the purpose of this exercise?" and "Bottom line, what exactly are we trying to achieve here?," which are precisely the kind of questions executive management wants every employee to ask. These are big picture questions.

Another way to think of this shift is to imagine that in the traditional task model, performing each high technology task is akin to putting the pieces together in a giant model of a building. Success is viewed as when the building model is done, with all the pieces in the right place. The focus here is on how good a shape the building model attains, not who or what makes it attain that shape.

In the new, task as an instrument model, each task is not just an activity of putting the pieces of a puzzle together. Rather, a task as an instrument has two components: first a task is a *tool* and second, the individual using this tool and making something with it. The individual uses this tool, engages in a constructive act, and gives it a shape by a steady process of *building*.

EXECUTION IS IN *HOW* AN INDIVIDUAL ACTS

To be sure, individuals in high technology companies undertake an extensive number of these high technology tasks every day. Activities such as product definition, interaction with customers, positioning the product in the competitive landscape, product planning, and so on, are what people do on a day-to-day basis.

However, neither the description of these activities, nor the degree of sophistication in how these activities are *formulated* determines the true success of a company.

On the contrary, the *execution quality*, the merit of how effectively a high technology group can lead the company towards success, emanates from the subterranean *individual tasks* that underlie each and every one of these activities. These tasks, and the individuals who perform these tasks, constitute the backbone of the execution engine of the company.

This is where the instrument-model of a task makes a difference. When a task is viewed as an activity with inputs and outputs, *performance* immediately takes the center stage, subverting the learning phase. Problems begin right away. Learning is relegated to an afterthought. The advantage in recasting the task as an instrument is, it is now easy to comprehend that for any execution to be effective, one must first learn to use this instrument skillfully.

A Matrix of Inter-related Purposes

At this time, a question raises itself regarding the nature of the forward movement. How do we recognize this forward movement? In what manner can we confirm that this forward movement is there and the company is moving along the right trajectory towards success?

The basic tenet in our approach is that we rooted this entire discussion on execution success in the basic experience of an individual. The key lies in recognizing that the forward movement from one context to another *is nothing but the forward movement engaged by each of us as individuals.*

A company's forward movement does not occur in vacuum. The forward movement in the contexts of a high technology enterprise is nothing but a dynamic coming together of individual forward movements that take place simultaneously in the enterprise. It is only when these individual forward movements are in a careful unison that the enterprise-wide forward movement from one context to another takes place.

For a technology executive, being involved in a leadership role should not amount to acting under the guiding principles of abstract, detached concepts, disconnected from his or her own personal world. On the contrary, the free-market context, in which the company finds itself in, is simply an extension of the changing experience which occur in each of us as individuals, as a result of what we *do*.

Of course it is true that at a first glance the high technology best practice concepts we read in books, and learn in training sessions, can be quite technical. But it is often the case that when these complex concepts are put into practice the level playing field boils down to the interaction of human beings against the background of their experience.

20

OVERCOMING TECHNOLOGY-CENTRIC VIEW

How is value created? What *is* value?

Quite often the meaning of the term "value" is quite murky. It stands for everything and nothing at the same time. When we say, "We need to build value" or "We should ensure that the product has economic value," we often confuse our listeners because they are not clear what we mean by "value."

Of course what come to our mind right-away are words such as "worth," the "utility" and "something of use." All these well-known meanings and interpretations are correct at a certain, *general* level.

Nevertheless, our mental image of the product actually *obscures and blocks us* from thinking clearly about the value of this product. Let us elaborate.

When we think of a typical engineered product, such as a computer or a mobile phone, we immediately think of this product in terms of its features, its shape and its color etc. And then we are reminded of how much we paid for it.

In our mind, this physical aspect, that which is tangibly visible is quite often tightly coupled with our recollection of what we *already* paid for it. In other words, the features and the contours of the physical product *are already priced in*. All that we can see in this product is merely the worth of what we paid for it. None of it is really *value*.

It is in this sense we say that the more you look at the product to look for value, the more you come away not knowing what the value is. So what is the value of a product?

The value of the product comes into view when we look *past* the engineered product that is in front of our eyes. When we go beyond all the complex technology behind the product and cast our glance *into the context* in which this product is used.

The basic thinking involved here is to recognize that everything that the company did to build this product in the technological context is *static*. The real economic value is a quality that comes forth only in the *forward movement* into the customer's overall system context. Let us illustrate this point.

THE QUALITY OF RELATEDNESS

One of the simplest day-to-day situations that brings home the phenomenon of value is when you look at an old calculator or that unused cassette tape player in your storage closet.

If value were to be a concrete thing residing in the actual device, independent of the customer context and depending only on the technological context, then the value must still exist in this device. As all the internal circuitry in this old device is still intact, you hear that crackling sound when you turn it on, then the value must still exist in this device. Isn't that so?

If value is a permanent thing born solely as a direct result of the efforts of the designers, the architects who originally designed, tested and qualified this device, then that value in this gadget should be as fresh and vibrant as it was at the time it was packaged, isn't it?

Then why is it that one finds this gadget in that old rusty closet? We should still be using this old gadget in our day to day activities today, just like we are using that latest PDA or the flat panel TV that we just bought.

The real reason is: the old gadget is in that closet because value does not lie in the actual product. It never did! The value, on the contrary, lies as the *quality of a relatedness* of the product to the individual user's interests. A value that is detached from this quality of relatedness *never had a permanent place* in any of the three contexts, even in the technological context.

At the time this old cassette tape player was designed and marketed, there indeed was a successful *transformation* from the technological context to the customer system context. As a consequence, there was indeed value to this product, otherwise as a consumer you wouldn't have bought it and enjoyed it as you did.

But the changing market conditions and the changing user preferences over time have exhausted the product's quality of relatedness. Now no matter how long you stare at it, you won't relate to it as a product that you want to use now. It is of no value to you, except as an antique. There is a memory of the value, but not a current utility.

TRACKING THE EXECUTION: A HYPOTHESIS

When we stop to think about it, in spite of our grand tour around the contexts, we still don't have a *measurable* grasp of what a successful execution in the company is. Is it because value itself is an immeasurable quantity? Hardly.

Companies are valued every day, as long as they are traded in a stock market, by that most specific and concrete value-carrier of all, the price of the company's stock. Not only that, every product a company makes is in turn valued by its customers, reflected in the product's price.

Regardless of the often-raised questions on a company's stock price, or on the justification for a product's high or low price, that the pricing mechanism, as a fair representation of the value, exists is in itself significant.

If price is such an ultimate antithesis of ambiguity, why can't we think of tracking the overall execution in a company along the same lines?

Let us consider the execution task of the product development and try to track this task, not from the project's progress, but from the *project's value contribution to the company.*

To this end, we are going to start with an imaginary stock market of a unique kind: a stock market for all products that are in development phase in the company. Here in this hypothetical stock market the ticker symbols represent the project names. Each project develops a product that eventually will go to market.

A HYPOTHETICAL STOCK EXCHANGE FOR PRODUCTS UNDER DEVELOPMENT

How does our hypothetical products stock market compare with the real stock market at exchanges such as NYSE™ or NASDAQ™?

A real stock market can be thought as an almost perfect *decentralized* decision making process in action. The owners of the stock do not *communicate* to each other. They are not *building* anything together that requires this communication.

Although the stock price is a representation of the collective decision on what price the stock is worth, there is no explicit coordination among these stock owners and traders. Hence this is a decentralized decision, arrived at independently by each stock owner and trader on what the individual thinks of the stock's value.

On the contrary, the execution task of the product development is replete with coordination. The nature of product development is such that there is a tremendous amount of communication involved among the development team members.

Imagine that we assign an initial price to the ticker symbols, each symbol representative of a distinct *product under development.* All the employees in the company, including those who are part of the engineering team, would then be allowed to trade in this hypothetical products stock market.

Companies which trade in real world stock markets exhibit business cycles. Likewise, the products under development, the entities behind the hypothetical product tickers in our hypothetical products stock market also exhibit cycles, except these are *product development cycles.*

Stock owners and traders in real world company tickers know that the price of the stock is a representation of the *economic value of the growth potential* of the company. This is regardless of what valuation measure is applied, such as a price-to-earnings ratio multiple, or the company's revenue growth.

What then, should the hypothetical ticker price represent in our hypothetical products stock market?

To answer this question, we need not look far beyond what we already know. *The hypothetical ticker price should be a measure of how strong the product's shift is, from the technological context to the economic context.*

In other words, the hypothetical ticker price should represent the *economic value added to* the product.

How is this economic value added to be interpreted? Let's try to construct a value model first.

First, what do we know about the current value of the project in which this product is being developed? All we know at this stage is the initial budget, i.e., the upfront estimates of all the design and development costs used in the budgetary planning of the engineering manager's project planning sheet.

That means that the current value of the product ticker is the sum total of all these fixed budgetary costs and *this is a negative quantity because it is a sunk cost.*

So the equation reads as follows:

the current value of the product ticker = negative fixed budgetary costs.

So what do we have here? A negative current value for the product ticker symbol!

There is only one way we can turn this negative quantity around: that is add another number to nullify and surpass this negative influence of the costs.

This positive number is the *economic value add*.

So we re-write this equation as follows:

the current value of the product ticker = economic value add + negative fixed budgetary costs

Factoring in the negative attribute of the fixed budgetary costs, we can rewrite the relation as:

the current value of the product ticker = economic value add <u>minus</u> fixed budgetary costs

Over time, when the collective product development team casts its eye on *building* the economic value add to this product, the current value of the product ticker will go positive.

Most product development managers, however, are fixated on keeping the second term on the right hand side fixed or keep it from growing. They forget that the key to success is *increasing the first term faster and sooner* than the second term.

If you are the project manager, managing the second term, the fixed budgetary costs, alone is not going to help. Moreover it gives *a false impression* that, the controlling of the second term and the mere passing of the time *somehow* come together into an increase in the current value of the product. But that is just what it is, a false impression. When this product goes to market, suddenly the market will tell you that all you did was to manage your costs, lost track of the economic value add and as a consequence *there is no economic value add* and the whole thing blows up in your face.

There is a sort of a resistance, a drag, a backwards pull, that is inherent in budget and planning-based activities of product development. While the value creating force looks forward and high, the budget looks *backward* and encourages hunkering down.

The market is full of potential and the only means to realize this potential is by giving in to the pull of the economic value add.

MARKETING: A UNIQUE FUNCTION

This statement may surprise the reader, but for most of us in the day-to-day busy-ness of the high technology world, the mental model of the company we carry in our heads is somewhat vague.

Whether we are engineers or marketers, our comprehension is fraught with our indecisive views on where exactly the contribution we make in the company is going. The value series that starts with our work, while clearly visible in the product that we design and bring to market, seems to terminate rather indiscriminately as it moves up the hierarchy.

In this vague awareness of the larger view, it is surprisingly easy to forget that a company is an independent entity. This vagueness seems to make us individuals a part of the company yet keep us invisible in the larger context with the same stroke.

When this happens, it seems to us that the company exists permanently, *without any relation to the decisions that we make* in our roles. The only time we think of the company *as an independent entity*, separate from us, is when a singularity event happens, like a threat to our career, a promotion or a bonus. Then we think of the other companies, automatically comparing our position vis-a-vis our friends at these companies.

But soon this active deliberation about the other possibilities dissipates and we once again fall into the day-to-day routine.

That vagueness is the death of the company. This is where the marketing role comes to rescue.

The marketing function in a high technology company sets the prevalent culture among its people, and the degree to which the employees feel the sense of urgency. The management's challenge is to infuse this sense of urgency without turning it into a panic-stricken seizure. There is always a danger that if overdone, fear takes over the very fabric of the day-to-day decision making function, tipping the company over. Many companies do exist in such seizure mode for years on.

In every one of these aspects, the marketing function plays a leading role. It provides the direction in the day-to-day workings. As a result, it is expressly important that the role of the marketing is understood clearly. With this in mind, we will take a closer look at the marketing function in the next, the final, chapter of this book.

21

MARKETING IS ORGANIZED DECISION MAKING

So we have come to the final chapter of our book. We have deliberately kept ourselves away from discussing the organization of the marketing function until the last stage.

It is our firm opinion that unless we *first* provide a comprehensive landscape of the underlying thinking, a discussion of the structural organization would be premature. We must first answer the question, "Why are things *this* way, and not *that* way?" Having dwelled on this question at length in the book until now, we are ready to say, "OK, so we know now what it is and why people behave that way. So, let's get down to understanding how a typical

marketing group is organized in a company to tackle these issues."
Our discussion in this chapter is centered on the marketing
function in a semiconductor company.

AN OVERVIEW

It is inconceivable to imagine an aspect of the high technology
company that is not touched by the marketing function. Every
company begins as a startup of one or the other kind. Some as a
spin-off from a larger entity and a still large number of them as new
startups. Whatever may be the genesis, a glimpse into the very first
business plan – the company pitch – clearly shows the importance
of the marketing chief's role.

As the funding is secured and the product is beginning to be
defined, product management function leads the charge into the
thick of the product development phase. Customer prospects are
engaged. Soon the public relations and marketing communication
groups start creating the presence of the company among the
industry peers. Applications engineering forms the hub for the
customer support, under the umbrella of the product management.

At this stage the company is in the playing field, provided the
promise of a working product is realistic. Strategic and tactical
marketing helps to maneuver the corporation in this playing field.
Product planning encompasses an entire course of activities from
the new product definition all the way to the product launch.
Operations is in full swing, performing the heavy weight tasks of
managing the supply chain. Customer marketing works hand in
hand with the sales channels, the eyes and ears of the company
listening and watching the customers.

These are the bulk of the marketing functions and roles we find
in any typical semiconductor company.

NO RULES

Underlying this broad sweep of the marketing roles, there are a set
of well-recognized high technology tasks. These are performed by

the individuals whose job it is to do these tasks in an effective manner to *execute* the marketing plan.

For example, in putting together the collateral for the press, the marketing communications team performs specific activities of editing the form and the content of the press releases to ensure that the collateral fits the target audience.

Often the semiconductor companies, especially those in the startup stages, have a tendency to market the data sheets, filling the press releases with excessive technical data which does not make any sense to the average person. A good marketing communications team avoids such pitfalls and works with the internal product management and design personnel to prune the data to articulate a clear and a specific message.

There are document deliverables attached to the product management function, deliverables such as the market requirements document, product manuals, marketing and product plan documents, forecasting spreadsheets, quarterly updates on the product development and so forth.

However, no one really learns all these tasks from a book. There are no rule books that lay out the procedures in preparing the deliverables. Unlike a design rule book that lays down the constraints in a chip design flow, there is no such equivalent guide for the inter-personal protocols that are implicitly understood and followed.

Nevertheless, most companies have tried and tested procedures, *ad hoc* they may be initially, that worked for them over a period of time. Over time, these procedures are winnowed and captured as *processes* which then serve as guidelines. Document templates are put in place to help perform these tasks.

BREAKING IT DOWN

A marketing group in a typical semiconductor chip company, with a system-on-a-chip IC as a main product, is chartered with the following activities as shown in the table.

Even as the table shows the *structure* of the marketing activities, it fails to capture an essential dimension that is an inherent part of

Marketing Roles in a Semiconductor Corporation

Strategy – Corporate, product, partnership. Differentiation, positioning. Roadmap – corporate, product, partnership. Identify new markets, define new products.	**Product Management** – Product profit and loss, marketing plans, market requirements. Manage cross functional teams – operations, finance, engineering, applications with support from legal	**Product Marketing** – Product definition, requirements, business case financials. Standards participation. Manage design-in programs. Manage OEM, ODM and CM relationships. Product planning
Tactical marketing – Competitive data gathering and analysis. Market research, market segmentation. Design partner programs. Lead generation – email marketing, direct mail, advertisements, webcasts etc. Product launch plans, customer profiles, track customer expectations and customer feedback	**Sales support** – Sales plans, sales training, field training. Support various sales staff – direct sales, field application engineers (FAE), sales reps, distributors. Manage channels – OEM, ODM, VAR and retail.	**Applications/Technical Marketing** – product demos, application notes, white papers, technical documentation, training materials
Marketing communications/PR – Co-marketing activities, collateral. Product releases – develop key messages to be communicated to the customer. Target technical, business press, investors, engineering and management community in the industry. Magazine articles, analyst briefings, presentations at tradeshows, conferences, industry panels etc. External marketing programs, web materials.		**Customer Marketing** – Forecasting, allocation, partnerships, delivery

the day-to-day marketing activities. Without the appreciation of this dimension, a real understanding of the semiconductor marketing is fruitless.

Semiconductor marketing is as much *an organized flow of information* as it is a structured organization. Individuals responsible must perform these tasks with an explicit eye to generate a useful body of information. This information is then used to make *decisions* by the team.

These decisions range anywhere from the choice of the particular trade show or a conference to set up a booth, the formation of a corporate strategy, to carefully positioning the company in the technical standards bodies and to the decision on how the next generation product should look like.

All such decisions, taken together, constitute the means by which the company steers itself in its progression towards a set goal. As the time passes and as the company gets closer to a working product, closer to the real possibility of a design win, the influence of each such decision made in the past becomes increasingly clear.

STRATEGY

Exactly what problem does the strategy function solve? One way to think of this sophisticated discipline is to first bring to our awareness *two essential absolutes* that are always breathing down the company.

VALUE CHAIN IS AN OPPORTUNITY

First, the chip company is not an economic entity in isolation but is an intricate part of a value chain: the OEMs that buy the chips from the chip company. The contract manufacturers, the distributors, the retail channel and the service providers that in turn channel the OEM's end products to end markets (to end customers.) To the extent that the OEMs, the channels and the end markets are instrumental in ensuring the customer-base for the chip company, they present *opportunities for the market share* to the chip company.

COMPETITION

The second absolute shows itself in the *competition*.

Simply put, whoever has an eye on any of your opportunity is your competition, fighting for the same market share.

Taken together, the opportunities and the competition represent an *active* environment that stands along the path of the company's progress.

But progress *to where*? And what does the strategy function has to do with this at all?

This brings us to the ultimate bedrock of any company's inner strength not only to survive but thrive well: the *vision* and the mission of the company.

VISION

The vision is the goal set in terms of the desired leadership qualities that the company aims to achieve.

The vision acts as a source of attraction set in the future and towards which the company, in its every manifestation, is moving. Every executive management presentation about the company starts with an articulation of what their vision for the company is. A mark of a good leadership is when the vision is cast as a corporate manifestation of every employee's urge to grow, to improve their own lives and the lives of the others around them.

When vision is cast this way, then the strategy serves the purpose of *clearing* of the path to progress towards realizing the vision.

The strategy function addresses the problem of how to maneuver the company in the midst of this active environment we described above.

At its core, the strategy function formulates a set of *actions* aimed at maximizing the opportunities and minimizing the competitive threats for increasing the company's market share.

Each time there is an increase in the market share as a result of putting this strategy function in play, the company is that much closer to realizing its vision.

IDENTIFY THE PROBLEM FIRST

It is important to remember that in *thinking* strategy, most successful high technology companies do not expect anyone to inform them of an identifiable market to start with.

Instead, what they look for is *an identifiable problem* that they can understand and articulate well.

In fact the thinking really starts with asking a question along the lines of: "How can we implement such and such in a better way, so that all these hundreds of steps the customer has to go through can be reduced to ten or twenty?"

Next question in the chain of thinking is: "When we *do* manage to reduce it to ten or twenty steps, what is the worth of this solution to the customer?"

This line of thinking continues with more hard line questions such as: Do we believe *and* can we confirm that the customer is willing to pay an extra premium every time he uses our solution, as a reward for you for easing their pain? If so, then can we quantify how much we can charge the customer?

Only when the company has quantitative answers to these questions, that it is convinced that it has makings of a new market. When the numbers are large enough to grab the management attention, then there is a chance to *create a new market*.

But that's not all. If you put yourself in the marketing's chief's shoes, this is how the thinking goes. You must test this new market segment against the longer term corporate vision of the company to see if there is an alignment.

For example, if the company's *vision* is to be among the top three semiconductor suppliers for wireless networks, then the company must ask: "If we invest time, money and resources to solve this problem, how does it help us to be a leading chip supplier to wireless networks?" If the company cannot find that connection then it must be aware of this disconnect and make appropriate decisions.

On the other hand, if there is indeed an alignment with the corporate vision and you decide to enter the market, there is a short initial period during which this new market can only be served by your solution. This crucial period represents a window of opportunity to solidify your presence in the market. Soon a competitor comes along and reduces this ten to twenty steps further down to one or two steps. Not only that, this competitor may afford to charge the customer less. When more and more competitors enter the market creating the downward spiral in the price, the innovative of the companies have already started to look elsewhere to build *next* new markets.

Strategy function encompasses all of the above. That questioning attitude, the articulation of the problem, quantifying the size of the ensuing market segment, weighing this market segment against the company vision, setting the roadmap for building the solution and finally crafting the solution into a product, all of it constitutes the strategy.

As you zero in from the market segment level viewpoint to the specific product-level scope in your questioning, the corporate strategy, the market strategy and the product strategy unravel to form a wholesome picture.

CORPORATE STRATEGY

To reiterate what we said earlier, the corporate strategy serves to maneuver the company on the path towards realizing the vision of the company.

For example, if the company's *vision* is to be among the top three semiconductor suppliers for wireless networks, then the corporate strategy is a *means* to get there. The corporate strategy should then be crafted such that it helps meet the required business, the financial and the market growth goals to be among the top three suppliers. The company could adopt the integrated device manufacturer approach, develop not only the system chip design but also the manufacturing of these chips.

Alternately the corporate strategy could be to adopt a fab-less semiconductor model with an exclusive focus on the wireless system IC market. Whatever be the corporate strategy, it must clearly set the company on the path towards realizing the vision.

From the marketing strategy standpoint, the company vision itself can be broken down into short term and longer term goals. For example if the vision is to be among the top three wireless semiconductor companies in five years from now, a corporate strategy can be crafted to target a two-year short term goal to be in the top ten list. Implicit in this kind of thinking is the realization that as the company evolves and matures in two years, it becomes increasingly capable of putting into play a much more aggressive strategy that propels it into a top-three slot.

MARKET STRATEGY

In reality it is *rarely* the case that a marketing team starts from scratch to formulate a market strategy, with no context whatsoever, with no product already in the development.

On the contrary, the context almost always is whatever the market segment for which there is an ongoing business activity in the company. Market strategy then becomes answering a question: "Where is our *next* opportunity and how do we play there?"

How does one begin to think, to identify this next opportunity?

During the initial stages of wrestling with this question, the issue is more of the thought and less of a process. What appears easily, prominently and without any effort in the thinking at this stage is that which is already most familiar: the product and the market segment that the company is *already* focusing on.

At the same time, being guided simply by the current market segment sometimes can cause a temporary blindness. It can block our vision from exploring the new market opportunities. This happens when all we can see are the problems with the current market segment.

Deteriorating pricing power, too many competitors, pitfalls and setbacks can be discouraging experiences. Self-doubts in one's own company's ability to execute can have a debilitating influence on the thinking.

This leads to a tendency to cast a wider fishing net, in a shot gun approach, to "mitigate risks," ignoring that the strength of any high technology product is differentiation and a focused approach to selected markets. In a way, all of this leads to a seizure of thinking in that it prevents us from even envisioning in our minds the next opportunity space. Eventually a failure of the will to succeed sets in.

When this happens, and precisely because these moments occur all too often in a marketer's mind, the big-picture corporate strategy should provide the anchor.

The twin entities of the corporate vision and the corporate strategy serve the purpose of rescuing the thinking from such seizures. The corporate vision provides a clear, unquestionable, solid identity as to *what we are as a company*. It says clearly that no we are not an entertainment company, not a wired communications company, nor are we a medical electronics company, but we are a semiconductor *chip* company with a specific focus on, for example, *wireless* networks.

IN CONCLUSION

So we have come to the end. In many ways, the approach followed in this book is an experiment. The notion of context developed in these pages is really an attempt to create a framework for learning. Learning, not in the conventional sense of knowledge and technique acquisition, but the acquisition of other people's *experience by the record of it*. The context space of semiconductor company execution is simply an application of the framework. We hope this approach and the high technology application gave the reader something useful to think about.

INDEX

INDEX

9 780387 233505